DID YOU KNOW?

A Collection of the Most Mind-Blowing Facts about Everything!

Over 1500 mind-blowing facts from history and science to pop culture and the absurd, these unbelievable truths will amaze, amuse, and leave you questioning reality!

DID
YOU KNOW?

A Collection of the Most Mind-Blowing Facts about Everything!

Over 1500 mind-blowing facts from history and science to pop culture and the absurd, these unbelievable truths will amaze, amuse, and leave you questioning reality!

Chris Guiher

Published by Clubhouse Publishing
This book is a work of non-fiction. While every effort has been made to ensure accuracy, the publisher and author make no warranties, express or implied, regarding the completeness, accuracy, or reliability of the information contained herein. The content is intended for entertainment and educational purposes only.

ISBN: 979-8-9868487-1-6

Dedication

To the endlessly curious—
the ones who ask "Why?"
and then ask "But why?" again.

To the trivia buffs, the fact hoarders,
and the people who know the capital of every country
but can't find their keys.

And to my family and friends—
thank you for tolerating my endless
"Did you know?" interruptions.

This book is for you.

DID YOU KNOW?

TABLE OF CONTENTS

Introduction

Welcome to the Realm of the Astonishing

Congratulations, intrepid reader! You've just opened a book that might very well blow your mind—or at least knock your socks off (no guarantees if you're reading this barefoot). What you hold in your hands is not just a collection of facts; it's a gateway to the weird, the wonderful, and the downright "Are you kidding me?" truths about the world we live in.

Ever wondered if history is hiding something bizarre? Spoiler alert: it absolutely is. Did you know Cleopatra lived closer to the invention of Snapchat than the building of the Great Pyramid? Or that octopuses might just be smarter than half your coworkers? (No offense to octopuses or your coworkers.) This book isn't here to answer *why* those things are true—it's here to revel in the sheer joy of discovering that they *are*.

Why a Book About Mind-Blowing Facts?

Good question, imaginary skeptical reader! We live in a world where curiosity often takes a backseat to cat videos and doomscrolling. But let's be honest—there's nothing quite like the thrill of learning something so utterly wild that you feel the urge to text your friends immediately (you might want to keep your phone handy for this).

This book was born out of a simple realization: the world is *bonkers*. From the deepest trenches of the ocean to the furthest reaches of space, life is brimming with surprises, many of which sound like they belong in a sci-fi movie or an episode of *The Twilight Zone*. The more I dug, the more I realized the facts don't just speak for themselves—they scream, whisper, and occasionally do a little dance.

How to Use This Book (Without Hurting Yourself)

This isn't the kind of book you need to read cover to cover. It's more of a buffet than a 10-course meal. Feel free to jump around, skip chapters, or stop halfway through a page to announce, "I had NO idea that was a thing!" (Your friends might get annoyed, but that's on them.)

The chapters are broken into themes to keep things organized. Love history? Dive into the stories of absurd coincidences and forgotten geniuses. Obsessed with space? There's a whole section dedicated to the stars, black holes, and the occasional exploding supernova. Or maybe you just want random trivia to win your next pub quiz—don't worry, I've got you covered there too.

What Makes a Fact "Mind-Blowing"?

Now, you might be wondering, "What exactly qualifies as a mind-blowing fact? Is there a committee?" (Sadly, no. Budget cuts.) For this book, it's anything that makes you stop and think, "Wait, *what?!*" It might be an unbelievable coincidence, a scientific discovery that feels like magic, or a piece of trivia that's so niche it should come with its own pair of nerd glasses.

Think of this book as your personal fact whisperer, here to remind you that the universe is vast, weird, and endlessly surprising. It's like a magic trick, except the magician is reality, and instead of pulling a rabbit out of a hat, it's pulling a jellyfish that can live forever.

A Warning (Kind Of)

Before we dive in, I should warn you: facts can be addictive. The more you know, the more you'll want to know, and soon you'll be that person at parties who says, "Did you know wombat poop is cube-shaped?" (It is, by the way, but you'll have to read the Nature chapter for details.)

The good news? This is the kind of addiction that makes you smarter, funnier, and much harder to beat at trivia night. So go ahead—embrace your inner nerd.

Let's Get Started

Are you ready to be amazed, entertained, and occasionally confused? Great! Let's journey through the quirks of history, the wonders of science, the secrets of pop culture, and everything in between.

You might laugh, you might gasp, and you might even roll your eyes. But if this book achieves one thing, I hope it reminds you how astonishing the world can be. After all, as Albert Einstein probably never said but should have: "Reality is weirder than fiction, and I'm totally here for it."

HISTORY'S ODDITIES

Surprising, quirky, and unbelievable moments from history.

Cleopatra lived closer to the Moon landing than the construction of the Great Pyramid.
The Great Pyramid was completed around 2560 BCE, while Cleopatra lived in 69 BCE. So, when she gazed at the pyramids, they were already ancient—more ancient to her than she is to us. Time is weird like that.

Napoleon was once attacked by rabbits.
The great military leader organized a rabbit hunt for himself and his men. Unfortunately, someone brought tame rabbits instead of wild ones, and they swarmed Napoleon thinking he was there to feed them. Strategy 0, rabbits 1.

The shortest war in history lasted only 38–45 minutes.
In 1896, Britain and the Sultanate of Zanzibar squared off in a conflict that was over before most people could finish lunch. The Sultan surrendered, and history promptly forgot the details.

Albert Einstein's brain was stolen.
After his death in 1955, a pathologist decided to keep Einstein's brain for "research." It was sliced into pieces and stored in jars. Turns out, you don't need to be a genius to commit medical theft.

In the 1920s, the U.S. government poisoned alcohol to discourage drinking during Prohibition.
When bootleggers continued to make liquor, the government added toxins to industrial alcohols to deter consumption. An estimated 10,000 people died. Talk about an over-the-top PSA.

A Roman emperor declared war on the sea.
Caligula, the famously eccentric emperor, once ordered his troops to attack the ocean. They gathered seashells as "spoils of war." It's unclear whether the ocean surrendered.

King Tut's dagger was made from a meteorite.
The teenage pharaoh's burial included a knife forged from extraterrestrial iron. Ancient Egyptians were clearly ahead of the cosmic curve.

The Great Fire of London in 1666 stopped the plague.
While devastating, the fire destroyed much of the city's rat-infested housing, effectively ending a plague outbreak. Sometimes, history has a strange way of solving its problems.

The Eiffel Tower was meant to be temporary.
Gustave Eiffel only built the iconic structure for the 1889 World's Fair. Parisians hated it, calling it an "eyesore," but it survived because dismantling it would have been more expensive.

The Boston Tea Party wasn't about tea taxes—it was about smuggling.
Many colonists were actually angry because the tax cut on British tea made it cheaper than smuggled Dutch tea. It was less a fight for liberty and more about market competition.

A man survived both atomic bombings in Japan.
Tsutomu Yamaguchi was in Hiroshima during the first bombing in 1945. He survived, went home to Nagasaki, and experienced the second bombing three days later. Despite this, he lived to the age of 93.

During the Great Emu War, Australia lost to birds.
In 1932, soldiers armed with machine guns tried to control an emu infestation in Western Australia. The emus outsmarted them at every turn, proving that even soldiers with guns can't always beat nature.

President Andrew Jackson had a 1,400-pound cheese wheel in the White House.
The wheel was a gift from New York farmers. When Jackson's term ended, he held a party where guests finished it off. Imagine the smell in the White House for weeks afterward.

The Library of Alexandria was destroyed multiple times.
Most people blame Julius Caesar's invasion, but scholars now believe the library was damaged in stages, with repeated fires, wars, and neglect. It's the historical equivalent of losing your USB drive repeatedly.

Paul Revere never shouted, "The British are coming!"
Why? Most colonial residents considered themselves British. Instead, he likely warned, "The Regulars are out," which doesn't have the same cinematic flair.

The ancient Romans used urine as mouthwash.
Its high ammonia content made it a surprisingly effective cleaning agent. However, no one knows who decided to try this first.

Anne Frank's diary was almost lost forever.
When the Nazis raided the annex, her notebooks were scattered. Miep Gies, a family friend, found them and kept them safe, never reading them out of respect.

The Colosseum could be flooded for naval battles.
The Romans ingeniously designed the Colosseum with systems to fill it with water, allowing mock naval battles. Imagine a combination of gladiator fights and *Pirates of the Mediterranean*.

Abraham Lincoln is enshrined in the Wrestling Hall of Fame.
Before becoming president, Lincoln had 300 wrestling matches under his belt and lost only one. Honest Abe could apparently throw down in the ring.

The inventor of the Pringles can is buried in one.
Fred Baur loved his creation so much that when he died, his family honored his request to have part of his ashes stored in a Pringles can.

The first bomb dropped on Berlin in World War II killed an elephant.
When the Allies began their air raids on Berlin, one of the earliest casualties was an elephant at the Berlin Zoo. History doesn't record whether the other animals were as unlucky.

Mozart once wrote a piece of music as a prank.
His *Musical Joke* was deliberately composed with off-key notes and awkward harmonies to mock less-skilled composers of the time. Even geniuses had a sense of humor.

The Leaning Tower of Pisa took nearly 200 years to complete.
Construction began in 1173, and it was already leaning before the third floor was finished. Despite its flaws, people in Pisa just decided to roll with it—for two centuries.

Medieval Europeans believed beavers could bite off their own testicles to escape hunters.
This myth became so widespread that beavers were often depicted performing this gruesome act in medieval artwork. Spoiler: it's not true.

The original name for the Statue of Liberty was "Liberty Enlightening the World."
While Americans affectionately call it the Statue of Liberty, its full title is far more grandiose. The French sure knew how to market their gifts.

The Great Wall of China isn't visible from space.
Despite the popular myth, astronauts have confirmed that it's nearly impossible to see the Wall with the naked eye. However, cities lit up at night? Very visible.

A chicken survived 18 months without a head.
In 1945, a farmer accidentally decapitated a chicken named Mike, but part of his brainstem remained intact. The bird became a sideshow star and lived for over a year on a diet of milk and grain fed directly into his throat.

Pope Gregory IX declared cats as agents of the devil.
This decree in the 13th century led to widespread cat massacres in Europe, which

may have indirectly contributed to the Black Plague by allowing rat populations to thrive. Way to go, Gregory.

The longest reigning monarch in history wasn't Queen Elizabeth II.
That title belongs to King Louis XIV of France, who ruled for 72 years and 110 days. He became king at the age of 4 and still managed to accomplish a lot—eventually.

The Eiffel Tower grows in summer.
Thanks to thermal expansion, the metal structure can grow up to 6 inches taller during hot weather. No wonder it's so iconic—it's a literal rising star.

The first known prosthetic was an Egyptian toe.
Archaeologists discovered a wooden toe on a mummy, proving that even 3,000 years ago, people were innovating ways to improve mobility.

There's a time capsule on the Moon.
Left by the Apollo 11 mission, it contains messages from world leaders and other artifacts intended to preserve a slice of humanity. Let's hope the aliens are good at reading microfilm.

A pigeon received a medal for bravery in World War II.
Cher Ami, a carrier pigeon, saved 194 soldiers by delivering a message despite being shot and severely injured. She was awarded the Croix de Guerre, proving that even pigeons can be heroes.

Shakespeare's parents were likely illiterate.
The man who enriched the English language with over 1,700 words probably didn't inherit his literary skills from Mom and Dad. Neither of them could sign their own names.

Thomas Edison didn't invent the lightbulb.
He perfected it. The idea had been around for decades, but Edison developed a practical, long-lasting bulb that changed the world. Marketing and timing are everything.

In ancient Egypt, servants were covered in honey to keep flies away from the pharaoh.
Talk about a sticky job. Being a royal was glamorous, but working for one? Not so much.

The Guinness Book of Records exists because of an argument.
Sir Hugh Beaver, the managing director of Guinness Breweries, couldn't settle a debate about the fastest game bird in Europe. He created the record book to prevent similar pub arguments.

A 10-day week once existed.
During the French Revolution, the calendar was changed to a 10-day week to de-Christianize timekeeping. Unsurprisingly, it didn't catch on, and people went back to the old seven-day routine.

Abraham Lincoln created the Secret Service the day he was assassinated.
Ironically, the Secret Service was formed to combat counterfeiting, not protect presidents. Their protective duties came much later.

The Liberty Bell cracked the first time it was rung.
Talk about starting on the wrong note. The bell has been recast multiple times but still cracked permanently after being rung for George Washington's birthday.

The Aztecs used cacao beans as currency.
Forget gold—chocolate was the real treasure. They traded beans for goods and services, which sounds like a delicious economy.

The largest diamond ever discovered was sent to England in a biscuit tin.
The Cullinan Diamond, weighing 3,106 carats, was so valuable that it was mailed in an unassuming tin to deter thieves. Imagine being the guy who almost ate it.

A French soldier fought in both the American and French Revolutions—and lived to see both World Wars.
Jean-Baptiste de Vimeur, Marquis de Rochambeau, served during the late 18th century, and while his active days of combat ended long before World War I, his incredibly long life made him a witness to remarkable shifts in global history.

The White House was almost painted black.
After being burned down by the British during the War of 1812, the White House was reconstructed and covered in white paint to hide burn marks. However, early discussions considered other colors, including yellow and gray.

Peter the Great taxed beards.
In an attempt to modernize Russia in the 1700s, Peter the Great instituted a beard tax. Men who wanted to keep their facial hair had to pay up and carry a "beard token" to prove they had paid.

A pope once put a dead pope on trial.
In 897 CE, Pope Stephen VI exhumed the body of his predecessor, Pope Formosus, and placed it on trial in the "Cadaver Synod." The corpse was found guilty, stripped of its papal garments, and unceremoniously thrown into the Tiber River.

The oldest "your mom" joke dates back to 1,500 BCE.
An ancient Babylonian tablet contains a joke about someone's mother. Even thousands of years ago, people couldn't resist a good (or bad) mom joke.

Thomas Jefferson invented the swivel chair.
The third U.S. president was not only a founding father but also an innovator. He designed a chair with a rotating seat, which he used while drafting the Declaration of Independence.

The Great Chicago Fire might have been started by a cow—but probably wasn't.
Legend has it that Mrs. O'Leary's cow kicked over a lantern, sparking the 1871 fire. However, historians now believe the real cause may have been careless humans—or even a meteor.

The ancient Romans had public toilets—but no toilet paper.
Instead, they used a communal sponge on a stick, rinsed in water between uses. Suddenly, history doesn't seem so glamorous.

Benjamin Franklin had a fake tombstone made for himself to prank tourists.
The stone read, "B. Franklin, Printer," and was installed years before his death. Franklin's humor apparently extended beyond his lifetime.

The Tower of London housed a polar bear.
In the 13th century, King Henry III received a polar bear as a gift from Norway. The bear lived at the Tower of London and was allowed to fish in the Thames River on a leash.

George Washington grew hemp—but not for smoking.
Hemp was a major crop in colonial America, used for rope, fabric, and paper. While Washington grew it at Mount Vernon, there's no evidence he ever rolled a joint.

The first Olympics in 776 BCE had only one event.
It was a short footrace of about 192 meters. No medals, no sponsors, and definitely no fancy opening ceremonies.

Joan of Arc's parents sued her hometown for her death.
Years after Joan was burned at the stake, her family sued the French government to clear her name. They won, though the victory was understandably bittersweet.

The first known vending machine dispensed holy water.
Invented by Hero of Alexandria in 1 CE, it required a coin to dispense a small amount of sacred water. Ancient innovation at its finest.

An English king ruled for only 20 minutes.
In 1483, King Edward V was technically king for about 20 minutes before his uncle, Richard III, seized the throne. His reign was shorter than most coffee breaks.

Ancient Egyptians loved their pets so much they mummified them.
From cats to monkeys to crocodiles, animals were embalmed and buried with their owners to accompany them into the afterlife. Clearly, pets have always been part of the family.

The U.S. accidentally bombed Canada in 1950.
During a training exercise, an American B-36 bomber mistakenly dropped a bomb near a remote Canadian village. Thankfully, it wasn't armed, but it left a large crater—and an awkward apology.

The Pentagon has twice as many bathrooms as necessary.
Built in the 1940s during segregation, the Pentagon was designed with separate

facilities for Black and white workers. Segregation ended before the building was completed, but the extra bathrooms remained.

A British soldier survived without food or water for seven days in the Sahara Desert.
During World War II, Corporal Bill Kennedy Shaw wandered the desert after being separated from his unit, surviving on dew collected from metal and eating buttons off his uniform.

Marie Antoinette's last words were an apology for stepping on her executioner's foot.
As she approached the guillotine, she accidentally stepped on the foot of her executioner and politely said, "Pardon me, sir, I did not mean to do it." Talk about staying classy under pressure.

The oldest known recipe is for beer.
A 4,000-year-old Sumerian tablet contains a detailed recipe for brewing beer. It's proof that humanity has always been good at prioritizing what matters most.

A Swedish king died from eating too much dessert.
King Adolf Frederick of Sweden died in 1771 after consuming a meal of lobster, caviar, champagne, and 14 servings of dessert. His cause of death? A literal food coma.

The world's first submarine attack happened during the American Revolution.
The Turtle, a small wooden submarine, attempted to attach a bomb to a British ship in 1776. It failed, but the idea was centuries ahead of its time.

The ancient Greeks used bread as an eraser.
Before the invention of rubber erasers, Greeks used pieces of bread to erase marks on papyrus. Imagine finishing your homework and having a snack at the same time.

A Japanese samurai once "fought" a duel with a wooden oar—and won.
Miyamoto Musashi, a legendary swordsman, famously defeated his opponent with a wooden oar he had carved into a makeshift sword. Talk about resourcefulness.

The world's longest chess match lasted over 20 hours.
In 1989, a chess game between Ivan Nikolic and Goran Arsovic lasted 269 moves before ending in a draw. It was less a game and more an endurance test.

The oldest known written complaint is about bad copper.
A Sumerian customer around 1750 BCE wrote a letter complaining about the poor quality of copper ingots he had received. History's first recorded "one-star review."

Thomas Edison proposed to his second wife in Morse code.
Edison taught his future wife, Mina, how to use Morse code so they could have private conversations. He then proposed by tapping out the words. Who needs a diamond when you've got dots and dashes?

Ancient Roman concrete is stronger than modern concrete.
Structures like the Colosseum and aqueducts have survived for millennia thanks to a volcanic ash mix that makes Roman concrete nearly indestructible. Modern engineers are still trying to replicate it.

A Polish doctor faked a typhus outbreak to save lives during World War II.
Dr. Eugene Lazowski created fake typhus test results to deter Nazis from entering Polish villages, saving hundreds of lives without firing a single shot.

The word "quarantine" comes from the Italian word for "forty."
Ships arriving in Venice during the Black Plague were required to anchor for 40 days to ensure they weren't carrying the disease. Hence, the term quarantine.

A dog was once the mayor of a town in Minnesota.
In the town of Cormorant, a Great Pyrenees named Duke was elected honorary mayor several times, proving that politics can go to the dogs—and it's still an improvement.

Julius Caesar was once captured by pirates—and demanded they raise his ransom.
When pirates kidnapped Caesar, they demanded 20 talents of silver for his release. He laughed, told them he was worth at least 50 talents, and ensured they raised the price. After his release, he returned with a fleet and had them all executed.

George Washington's teeth weren't made of wood.
Despite popular belief, his dentures were made from a combination of human teeth, animal teeth, and ivory. Still not great, but slightly less splintery.

The Eiffel Tower was almost dismantled and sold for scrap.
In 1909, the Tower's 20-year lease was about to expire, and Parisians debated tearing it down. Gustave Eiffel himself had to step in to save his creation.

In 1518, a "dancing plague" took over a French town.
Dozens of people in Strasbourg began dancing uncontrollably for days, some until they collapsed or died. The cause remains unknown, but it's one of history's weirdest medical mysteries.

Genghis Khan's empire was so vast it connected the East and West.
The Mongol Empire created the first international postal system and facilitated trade along the Silk Road. Who knew the guy who conquered most of Asia also streamlined mail delivery?

An emperor made his horse a senator.
Caligula, ever the eccentric, appointed his favorite horse, Incitatus, to the Roman Senate. While it might seem bizarre, it's worth noting the horse probably made fewer bad decisions than some human senators.

The first speeding ticket was issued in 1896.
A man in London was fined for going 8 mph in a 2 mph zone. The "high-speed chase" involved a constable on a bicycle.

The ancient Mayans invented bubble gum.
They used chicle, a natural gum from tree sap, for chewing and adhesive purposes. Modern chewing gum owes its origins to these ancient innovators.

Pope John XII died in bed—with someone else's wife.
One of the most scandalous popes in history, John XII met his end under questionable circumstances during an affair. The Vatican probably didn't advertise this in Sunday school.

NATURE'S WONDERS

Astonishing facts about animals, plants, and natural phenomena.

Sharks have existed longer than trees.
Sharks have been roaming the oceans for over 400 million years, while trees didn't appear until about 350 million years ago. Next time you see a shark, remember you're looking at a living fossil that predates forests.

Octopuses have three hearts and blue blood.
Two hearts pump blood to the gills, and one pumps it to the rest of the body. Oh, and

their blood is copper-based, giving it a blue hue. Basically, they're nature's alien overlords.

Sloths can hold their breath longer than dolphins.
While dolphins can hold their breath for about 10 minutes, sloths can slow their heart rate and hold theirs for up to 40 minutes. Not bad for a creature that moves slower than your morning commute.

The Amazon rainforest produces 20% of the world's oxygen.
Known as the "lungs of the Earth," the Amazon plays a crucial role in regulating our planet's atmosphere. Unfortunately, deforestation is threatening this natural wonder.

A jellyfish has lived for millions of years without a brain.
The *Turritopsis dohrnii*, also known as the immortal jellyfish, can revert its cells to an earlier stage and essentially live forever. It doesn't even need a brain to outsmart death.

Wombat poop is cube-shaped.
This bizarre fact isn't just for laughs—scientists believe the unusual shape helps the poop stay in place and mark territory without rolling away. It's nature's version of Lego.

The ocean contains 20 million tons of gold.
While it's scattered in microscopic particles, the sheer amount of gold dissolved in seawater is mind-boggling. If only there were a way to mine it without bankrupting yourself.

A species of fungus can take over ants' minds.
The *Ophiocordyceps unilateralis* fungus infects ants, controls their behavior, and forces them to climb to a high spot where the fungus can spread its spores. Nature isn't just beautiful—it's terrifying.

Elephants mourn their dead.

Elephants have been observed grieving over the bones of their kin, touching them gently with their trunks. Some even shed tears. Who knew these gentle giants were so emotionally deep?

There's a plant that can "remember" and "learn."

The Mimosa pudica, also known as the "sensitive plant," closes its leaves when touched. In experiments, it learned to stop reacting to non-harmful touches, showing a surprising level of plant "memory."

The Earth's core is hotter than the surface of the Sun.

While the Sun's surface is about 10,000°F, the Earth's core is estimated to be over 10,800°F. It's like having a star right beneath our feet.

Bananas are berries, but strawberries aren't.

Botanically speaking, a berry must develop from a single ovary and have seeds inside. Bananas check all the boxes, while strawberries break the rules. Mother Nature clearly doesn't follow grocery store logic.

Ants outnumber humans a million to one.

There are approximately 20 quadrillion ants on Earth. That's 20,000,000,000,000,000 ants—or more than a few picnic invaders per person.

A single tree can drink 100 gallons of water a day.

Large trees like oaks can absorb and circulate about 100 gallons of water from the ground to their leaves every single day. That's like a tree-sized water bottle on steroids.

The Arctic reindeer's eyes change color.
In summer, their eyes are golden, but in winter, they turn blue to help them see in low light. That's the kind of cool trick even humans would envy.

Penguins propose with pebbles.
Male penguins find the smoothest, most perfect pebble and present it to their chosen mate. If she accepts, they're officially a couple. Basically, it's nature's cutest engagement ritual.

Coral reefs are the largest structures made by living organisms.
The Great Barrier Reef is visible from space and spans over 1,400 miles. It's essentially an underwater city, teeming with marine life.

Butterflies taste with their feet.
Their feet have sensors that allow them to "taste" whatever they land on. Imagine walking across your dinner to see if it's worth eating.

Some trees can clone themselves for thousands of years.
The Pando tree colony in Utah is one of the oldest living organisms on Earth, estimated to be around 80,000 years old. It's essentially a forest of clones, all connected by a single root system.

Crows can remember faces and hold grudges.
Studies show crows can recognize human faces and even teach their offspring to avoid certain people. Basically, don't mess with a crow unless you want an entire murder of them after you.

A blue whale's heart is the size of a small car.
Weighing about 400 pounds, a blue whale's heart is massive enough that a human could crawl through its arteries. Talk about wearing your heart on your sleeve—or in the ocean.

Earth's magnetic field is flipping.
Scientists believe the planet's magnetic poles are gradually reversing—a process that takes thousands of years. When it's complete, compasses will point south instead of north. Chaos for mapmakers, fun for the rest of us.

There's a hidden underground rainforest in China.
A giant sinkhole in Guangxi, China, revealed a lush forest inside, complete with trees up to 130 feet tall. It's like something out of *Jurassic Park*—minus the dinosaurs (so far).

Cows have best friends.
Research has shown that cows form close bonds with other cows, and they become stressed when separated. Friendship: not just for humans.

Sea otters hold hands while they sleep.
To keep from drifting apart, sea otters float on their backs and hold paws. It's not just practical—it's heart-meltingly adorable.

The northern lights make noise.
Auroras are often accompanied by faint, crackling sounds that scientists believe are caused by charged particles colliding in the atmosphere. Nature's light show has a soundtrack.

A cockroach can live for weeks without its head.
Since cockroaches breathe through small holes in their body segments and don't rely on their head to survive, they can keep scuttling around—until they die of thirst. Creepy but true.

Sea cucumbers can eject their organs as a defense mechanism.
When threatened, sea cucumbers can literally spill their guts to distract predators and then regenerate their organs later. Nature's version of "out of sight, out of mind."

A single lightning bolt is five times hotter than the surface of the Sun.
A lightning bolt can reach temperatures of 50,000°F. So when it lights up the sky, it's not just dazzling—it's cooking the air.

There are more trees on Earth than stars in the Milky Way.
Earth is home to about 3 trillion trees, compared to the Milky Way's estimated 100 billion stars. Turns out, we live in a very leafy galaxy.

Goats have rectangular pupils.
Their strange, horizontal pupils give them panoramic vision, which helps them spot predators. Fashionable and functional.

Jellyfish existed before dinosaurs.
Some species of jellyfish have been floating around Earth's oceans for over 500 million years, making them older than sharks, trees, and dinosaurs combined.

Honey never spoils.
Archaeologists have found pots of honey in ancient Egyptian tombs that are over 3,000 years old—and still perfectly edible. Sweet preservation at its finest.

Kangaroos can't walk backward.
Thanks to their muscular tails and body structure, kangaroos can only move forward. It's like they're permanently committed to progress.

Whale songs can travel thousands of miles underwater.
Humpback whales' songs can be heard by other whales over 3,000 miles away, making them the ocean's original long-distance communicators.

A sunflower isn't a single flower.
What looks like one flower is actually a cluster of thousands of tiny flowers, called florets, arranged in a mesmerizing spiral pattern.

The Antarctic ice sheet contains about 60% of the world's fresh water.
If it melted completely, global sea levels would rise by about 200 feet. Talk about an icy giant with global impact.

The peregrine falcon is the fastest animal on Earth.
It can dive at speeds of over 240 mph, making it faster than a Formula 1 car and any land animal. Talk about breaking the speed limit.

There are rivers beneath the ocean.
Underwater currents, known as submarine rivers, flow through the deep ocean, carrying water denser with sediment than the surrounding seawater. It's like a hidden world within a hidden world.

Spiders can fly using electricity.
Some species of spiders release silk into the air and use the Earth's electric field to lift themselves off the ground, traveling hundreds of miles. Creepy, but impressive.

The "immortal" bristlecone pine tree is over 5,000 years old.
These ancient trees, found in California, have witnessed millennia of history and remain some of the oldest living organisms on Earth.

A group of flamingos is called a "flamboyance."
With their bright pink feathers and graceful stance, it's a name that fits perfectly.

Antarctica is technically a desert.
Despite being covered in ice, Antarctica gets less precipitation annually than the Sahara Desert, making it one of the driest places on Earth.

Sea sponges are technically animals.
They might not look like much, but sea sponges are classified as animals, not plants, because they feed on organic material and lack chlorophyll.

Earth's rotation is slowing down.
The planet's rotation slows by about 1.7 milliseconds per century due to the gravitational pull of the Moon. In about a few billion years, our days might be 25 hours long.

Giant pandas can fake pregnancy.
Female pandas have been known to exhibit signs of pregnancy—like eating more and moving less—to get extra care and food from zookeepers. Sneaky, but genius.

Some frogs freeze solid and come back to life.
Certain species, like the wood frog, can survive freezing temperatures by essentially shutting down their bodies, only to thaw out and hop away in the spring.

A tiger's skin is striped, just like its fur.
Even if you shaved a tiger, you'd still see its distinctive stripes. The pattern is as unique as a fingerprint.

Bees can recognize human faces.
Bees use a technique called "configural processing" to distinguish faces, much like humans do. Who knew they were such great social observers?

Volcanoes can "sing."
Some volcanoes emit low-frequency sounds, or "infrasound," that can't be heard by the human ear but can be detected with specialized equipment. It's like Earth's own eerie soundtrack.

Albatrosses can fly for years without landing.
These seabirds can stay airborne for years, using wind currents to glide effortlessly. Talk about taking the scenic route.

Lobsters taste with their legs.
Their tiny hair-covered appendages can detect chemicals in the water, helping them "taste" their surroundings before committing to a meal.

Crocodiles can climb trees.
While they might not seem agile, crocodiles have been observed climbing trees to bask in the sun or survey their surroundings. Yet another reason to avoid treehouses near swamps.

Some fish can walk on land.
The mudskipper, a fish that can breathe through its skin and fins, is perfectly capable of crawling on land. Evolution, take a bow.

Venus flytraps count their prey.
They don't snap shut until triggered twice by a potential meal, ensuring they don't waste energy on false alarms. Efficiency is key, even in carnivorous plants.

Fire ants can form rafts to survive floods.
By linking their bodies together, fire ants create floating colonies that can last for weeks. It's teamwork at its most terrifying.

Polar bears have black skin under their white fur.
The black skin helps them absorb and retain heat, while their seemingly white fur is actually translucent, reflecting the light.

A shrimp's heart is in its head.
Literally. Their hearts are located near their brains, making them creatures that truly "think with their heart."

Quokkas are the happiest-looking animals on Earth.
Known for their seemingly constant smiles, these small marsupials are so cheerful-looking that they've become social media stars.

Beetles account for 25% of all known life forms.
With over 400,000 species identified, beetles are the most diverse group of animals on Earth. Nature must really love beetles.

Caterpillars turn to goo in their cocoons.
During metamorphosis, they break down into a soup-like substance before reassembling into a butterfly. It's transformation in its messiest form.

The Sahara Desert was once a lush, green paradise.
Around 10,000 years ago, the Sahara was covered in lakes, rivers, and grasslands. Climate change over millennia turned it into the vast desert we know today.

Some flowers bloom only at night.
The moonflower and the queen of the night cactus open their petals after sunset, often filling the night air with enchanting fragrances.

Peacocks shed their feathers every year.
Those stunning tail feathers don't last forever. Each year, peacocks lose their plumage, only to grow new ones during the next mating season.

Ostriches can run faster than horses.
Reaching speeds of up to 60 mph in short bursts, these flightless birds are built for sprinting.

The largest living organism is a fungus.
A single honey fungus in Oregon spans over 2.4 miles underground, making it the largest living organism on Earth.

The planet's longest-living creature is a sponge.
Certain Antarctic sponges are estimated to be over 10,000 years old. Take that, Methuselah!

Starfish have no brains or blood.
They use filtered seawater instead of blood and rely on a nerve ring to sense their surroundings. Minimalist biology at its finest.

Rats laugh when tickled.
Yes, you read that right. Rats emit high-frequency giggles when tickled, but you'll need specialized equipment to hear them.

Some turtles breathe through their butts.
Known as cloacal respiration, this ability allows certain turtles, like the Australian Fitzroy River turtle, to extract oxygen from water using specialized structures in their rear. Talk about a unique survival skill.

Ravens can imitate human speech.
Like parrots, ravens are excellent mimics and can learn to repeat words and sounds, often surprising their human companions with their intelligence.

The pangolin is the only mammal with scales.
Covered in hard keratin scales, pangolins use these protective shields to roll into a ball when threatened. Sadly, they're also the most trafficked mammal in the world.

Sea stars can regenerate lost arms.
If a sea star loses an arm, it can grow a new one. In some cases, a lost arm can even grow into an entirely new sea star. Nature truly doesn't waste anything.

The smell of freshly cut grass is a plant distress signal.
That nostalgic scent of a mowed lawn? It's actually grass releasing chemicals to signal injury and call for help—though there's not much it can do about your lawnmower.

Snowflakes aren't completely unique.
While it's rare, studies have shown that snowflakes can form identical structures under the right conditions. So much for "one in a million."

The Greenland shark can live for centuries.
These deep-sea giants can live for up to 500 years, making them one of the longest-living vertebrates on Earth. Some of the older sharks were likely born during the Renaissance.

The Amazon River once flowed in the opposite direction.
Millions of years ago, the Amazon flowed from east to west, but the rise of the Andes Mountains reversed its course. Mother Nature really flipped the script.

Birds don't pee.
Instead of urine, birds excrete a white paste called uric acid. Their all-in-one waste system is efficient—if not always convenient for your car.

Cows produce more milk when they listen to music.
Studies have found that playing relaxing music, like classical tunes, can increase milk production in cows. Who knew Beethoven could boost dairy output?

There's a "blue hole" in Belize that's 400 feet deep.
The Great Blue Hole is a giant underwater sinkhole off the coast of Belize that's so large it can be seen from space. It's one of the ocean's greatest mysteries.

Caterpillars have more muscles than humans.
With over 4,000 muscles in their tiny bodies, caterpillars have incredible control over their movement. For comparison, humans only have around 600 muscles.

Slime molds can solve mazes.
Despite having no brain, slime molds can find the shortest path through a maze to reach food. Scientists are even studying them for insights into network optimization.

Earth has its own "heartbeat."
Known as the Schumann resonance, the planet emits electromagnetic waves that pulse at 7.83 Hz, creating what some call Earth's natural rhythm.

Dragonflies are expert hunters.
With a hunting success rate of 95%, dragonflies are among the most efficient predators in the animal kingdom, capturing their prey mid-flight with surgical precision.

The oldest fossils are 3.5 billion years old.
These ancient cyanobacteria fossils were found in Australia, offering a glimpse into Earth's earliest life forms. That's way older than your grandma's favorite recipe.

Some lakes can explode.
Lakes like Lake Nyos in Cameroon contain layers of carbon dioxide that can suddenly erupt, releasing deadly gas clouds. It's called a limnic eruption, and it's as terrifying as it sounds.

Giant squids have eyes as big as basketballs.
Their massive eyes help them spot predators like sperm whales in the pitch-black depths of the ocean. It's nature's version of night vision goggles.

A group of owls is called a "parliament."
It's a fitting name for these wise-looking birds, though they probably make decisions faster than most human parliaments.

Polar bears overheat more easily than they freeze.
Despite their icy habitats, polar bears are so well-insulated by fur and fat that they can overheat if they run or exert themselves too much.

Ants can carry up to 50 times their body weight.
These tiny insects are the ultimate weightlifters, capable of hauling objects much larger than themselves. If humans had this strength, we'd be lifting cars like dumbbells.

Dolphins have names for each other.
Dolphins use unique whistles to identify and call to each other, essentially giving themselves names. It's like having underwater Twitter handles.

The Earth's clouds weigh billions of tons.
A typical cumulus cloud contains about a million pounds of water. Fortunately, that weight is spread out enough to float in the sky.

Mantis shrimp punch so hard they boil water.
These small, colorful creatures can punch with such force that they create tiny bubbles of boiling water, capable of stunning prey—or breaking aquarium glass.

A lion's roar can be heard from five miles away.
Their powerful roar serves as a long-distance communication tool, letting rivals know who's boss from miles around.

Some fish glow in the dark.
Bioluminescent fish like the flashlight fish use light-producing bacteria to create their eerie glow. It's like having a built-in nightlight.

There are more microorganisms in a teaspoon of soil than there are people on Earth.
Each teaspoon contains billions of bacteria, fungi, and other microscopic life forms. So, the next time you see dirt, think of it as nature's bustling metropolis.

THE HUMAN BODY

Mind-blowing truths about human biology and capabilities.

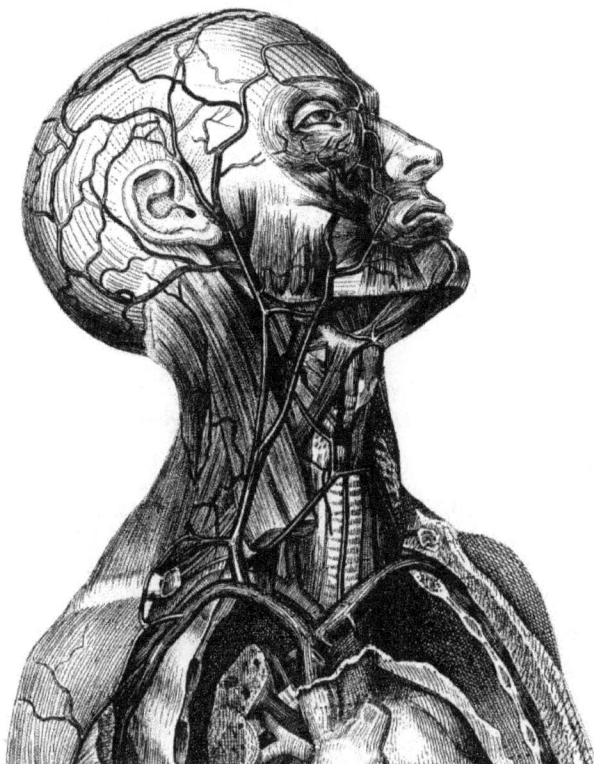

Your brain generates enough electricity to power a light bulb.
The human brain produces about 12–25 watts of electricity, which is enough to light a small bulb. You're literally thinking in energy.

Your stomach gets a new lining every 3–4 days.
Without this regular replacement, the acids in your stomach, which are strong enough to dissolve metal, would digest your own body.

You're taller in the morning than at night.
Gravity compresses the cartilage in your spine throughout the day, making you slightly shorter by bedtime. Morning you is about half an inch taller.

Your heart beats over 100,000 times a day.
This vital organ pumps blood through 60,000 miles of blood vessels—enough to circle the Earth more than twice.

Your liver can regenerate itself.
The liver is the only organ that can regenerate, even if as much as 75% of it is removed. It's basically the Wolverine of your body.

Your nose can detect about 1 trillion different scents.
Once thought to detect just 10,000 scents, recent studies have revealed the human nose is far more powerful—though some smells we'd rather avoid.

Humans have fewer muscles than caterpillars.
While we have about 600 muscles, caterpillars boast over 4,000. Thankfully, they don't need gym memberships.

Your blood travels 12,000 miles a day.
That's the equivalent of flying from New York to Sydney and back twice—all happening inside your veins.

Your bones are five times stronger than steel.
Ounce for ounce, human bones are stronger than steel but are also lightweight, making them perfect for structural support.

You produce enough saliva in a lifetime to fill two swimming pools.
The average person produces about 25,000 quarts of saliva over their lifetime, which is both fascinating and mildly unsettling.

Goosebumps are a leftover from evolution.
They were once useful for making our ancestors' hair stand on end, helping them appear larger to predators. Now they just show up when we're cold or emotional.

Your body has more bacteria than human cells.
You're made up of about 37 trillion human cells but host around 39 trillion bacterial cells. You're more microbe than human.

Your tongue is the strongest muscle relative to its size.
While small, the tongue works tirelessly, helping us speak, eat, and swallow. Give it some credit—it never takes a day off.

Your skin sheds about 1.5 pounds of cells a year.
That dust in your home? A good portion of it is likely dead skin cells. You're constantly leaving a little bit of yourself everywhere.

Your bones are constantly being rebuilt.
Every 10 years or so, your skeleton essentially replaces itself as old bone cells are broken down and replaced with new ones.

You can live without a stomach.
Though vital for digestion, people can survive without a stomach thanks to modern medicine, as other parts of the digestive system adapt to compensate.

Your heart has its own electrical system.
Even if disconnected from your body, your heart can keep beating for a short time as long as it has oxygen.

Your brain doesn't feel pain.
While it processes pain signals from the rest of the body, the brain itself lacks pain receptors, which is why brain surgeries can sometimes be performed while the patient is awake.

Your eyes can distinguish about 10 million colors.
The human eye is incredibly sensitive, capable of perceiving an astonishing range of colors—even if we struggle to name them all.

You shed about 50–100 hairs a day.
Before you panic, that's normal! With over 100,000 hair follicles on your scalp, this daily loss is barely noticeable.

Your gut is home to over 100 million neurons.
Often called the "second brain," your gut's complex nervous system helps control digestion and even impacts your mood.

Your sense of taste is 80% smell.
Without your nose, most foods would taste bland. Try holding your nose the next time you eat something—it's a whole different experience.

Humans glow in the dark.
Bioluminescence isn't just for fireflies. Humans emit a faint light, invisible to the naked eye, due to chemical reactions in our cells.

Your fingerprints form before you're born.
By the 10th week of pregnancy, a fetus already has its unique set of fingerprints. Talk about an early signature.

The acid in your stomach could dissolve razor blades.
Thankfully, your stomach lining protects you from this powerful digestive acid. It's like having a little chemistry lab inside you.

Your brain uses about 20% of your body's energy.
Despite making up only 2% of your body weight, your brain is a power-hungry organ, burning through glucose like there's no tomorrow.

Your nails grow faster on your dominant hand.
So, if you're right-handed, your right-hand nails grow slightly faster. Maybe it's all that extra typing and gesturing.

You can't tickle yourself.
Your brain knows what's coming when you try, so it doesn't react the same way as when someone else tickles you. Nice try, though.

Your lungs are covered in tiny hair-like structures.
Called cilia, these structures help clear mucus and debris from your respiratory system. They're like janitors for your lungs.

You lose 90% of your body heat through your head.
That's why wearing a hat is so effective in keeping you warm. Your brain might not feel pain, but it sure does love staying toasty.

Your blood is red because of iron.
The iron in hemoglobin, which carries oxygen in your blood, gives it its characteristic red color. Without iron, your blood wouldn't be nearly as vibrant.

You blink about 15–20 times per minute.
That's about 1,200 times an hour or 28,800 times a day. Blinking is your body's way of keeping your eyes clean and moist.

Humans can survive without a spleen.
While important for filtering blood and fighting infections, the spleen isn't essential, and other organs can take over its functions if needed.

Your ears and nose never stop growing.
Unlike bones, cartilage continues to grow throughout your life, which is why older people often have larger ears and noses.

Yawning cools your brain.
It's not just a sign of tiredness—yawning helps regulate brain temperature, acting like a natural fan for your head.

Babies are born with about 300 bones.
As they grow, some of these bones fuse together, leaving adults with 206. It's a literal case of quality over quantity.

Your blood makes up about 8% of your body weight.
That's roughly 1.2–1.5 gallons of blood circulating through the average adult's veins and arteries. That's a lot of life juice.

You technically only need one lung.
While it wouldn't be ideal, you could live with just one lung, as it would expand to compensate for the missing one.

Your body replaces millions of cells every second.
In the time it took you to read this sentence, millions of your cells have been replaced, keeping you alive and functional.

The average human body contains about 37.2 trillion cells.
Each of those cells is a tiny universe working in harmony to keep you going. It's mind-blowing when you think about it.

Human DNA is 98.8% identical to chimpanzee DNA.
We share nearly all of our genetic code with our closest relatives. That remaining 1.2% makes all the difference.

Your pinky finger accounts for 50% of your hand's strength.
Despite its small size, your pinky is a powerhouse, contributing significantly to grip and hand function.

Your skin is your largest organ.
Stretching out to about 22 square feet on the average adult, your skin is a protective barrier, temperature regulator, and sensory organ all rolled into one.

Your bones are hollow yet incredibly strong.
The hollow structure makes them lightweight, while their internal lattice structure provides strength and durability—nature's perfect design.

You can survive for weeks without food, but only days without water.
While your body can break down fat and muscle for energy, it cannot function without water to regulate temperature and maintain organ health.

Your eyes are the second most complex organ after the brain.
They can adjust focus between objects at different distances in less than a second, a feat that no camera can replicate perfectly.

You blink more when you're talking.
Studies show that people blink more frequently when speaking than when listening. It's like your body's punctuation.

Your ears are always working—even when you sleep.
While your brain tunes out most sounds during sleep, your ears continue to pick up noises, ready to alert you if something is amiss.

Your bones are constantly under construction.
Osteoclasts break down old bone tissue, while osteoblasts build new bone. This remodeling process ensures your skeleton stays strong and healthy.

The human brain has about 86 billion neurons.
Each neuron can connect to thousands of others, creating an intricate network responsible for everything you think, feel, and do.

Your eyelashes have a lifespan of about 3 months.
After growing for about 30 days, an eyelash lives for 2 months before falling out and being replaced.

Your body temperature peaks in the late afternoon.
Circadian rhythms cause your temperature to rise throughout the day, hitting its highest point around 4–6 PM.

You lose about 30,000 to 40,000 skin cells every minute.
That's roughly 50 million cells a day, making your skin a constant work-in-progress.

Your brain processes information at an estimated 120 meters per second.
That's faster than a Formula 1 car at full speed, enabling you to react almost instantly to stimuli.

Your teeth are harder than your bones.
The enamel on your teeth is the hardest substance in your body, built to withstand years of chewing and grinding.

Your body produces 25 million new cells every second.
In the time it takes to read this fact, your body has replaced millions of old cells with new ones.

The human nose can detect emotions.
Studies suggest that humans can smell emotions like fear and happiness through subtle chemical signals emitted by the body.

Your blood vessels could circle the Earth twice.
If laid end to end, the network of blood vessels in your body would stretch about 60,000 miles—enough to wrap around the planet multiple times.

You're more likely to have a heart attack on a Monday.
Stress and changes in routine make Monday mornings statistically more dangerous for heart health. Another reason to dislike Mondays.

The muscles that control your eyes are the most active in your body.
They move more than 100,000 times a day to focus and adjust your vision, making them incredibly hardworking.

Your nails grow faster in the summer.
Warm weather and increased blood flow during the summer months accelerate nail growth.

The average adult has about 4–6 liters of blood.
This essential fluid accounts for roughly 7–8% of your total body weight, keeping your organs and tissues nourished.

You have unique tongue prints.
Just like fingerprints, your tongue has a one-of-a-kind pattern that could theoretically be used for identification.

Your brain shrinks as you age.
Starting in your 30s or 40s, your brain loses about 1% of its volume each year, though this doesn't necessarily affect intelligence.

Your ears help you balance.
The inner ear contains tiny structures called semicircular canals that detect changes in motion and position, helping you stay upright.

The human body contains trace amounts of gold.
While it's not enough to make you rich, about 0.2 milligrams of gold can be found in your blood, mainly in the joints.

Your hair grows about 6 inches a year.
On average, human hair grows about half an inch per month, making it one of the fastest-growing tissues in the body.

The average person walks the equivalent of 5 times around the Earth in their lifetime.
Over 75 years, you'll likely cover more than 110,000 miles on foot—talk about mileage!

Your body produces about a liter of mucus every day.
It might sound gross, but mucus plays a vital role in trapping bacteria and keeping your respiratory system moist.

Babies have around 10,000 taste buds.
This is far more than adults, as taste buds diminish with age, making childhood the height of flavor sensitivity.

Your brain can store about 2.5 petabytes of information.
That's roughly the same as 3 million hours of TV shows—though you probably won't remember the ending of half of them.

Your body can survive without some major organs.
People can live without a spleen, gallbladder, appendix, and even one kidney or lung. Your body is great at adapting to loss.

Your digestive system is about 30 feet long.
From your mouth to your anus, this long and winding system ensures nutrients are absorbed and waste is expelled.

You spend about 5 years of your life eating.
Between cooking, chewing, and swallowing, the average person devotes nearly 43,800 hours to food consumption.

Your heart beats about 3 billion times in a lifetime.
Assuming an average lifespan of 75 years, that's a whole lot of thumping.

Your body temperature drops when you sleep.
This natural cooling process helps conserve energy and signals your brain that it's time to rest.

Humans are bioluminescent, but it's invisible.
Your body emits faint light as a byproduct of cellular processes, though it's about 1,000 times weaker than what the human eye can detect.

Your kidneys filter about 50 gallons of blood daily.
These vital organs work tirelessly to remove toxins and maintain your body's fluid balance.

You produce about 1.5 pints of sweat daily.
Sweating helps regulate your body temperature, even if it's not always socially convenient.

Your brain doesn't multitask.
Despite what you might think, your brain switches rapidly between tasks rather than focusing on multiple things simultaneously.

Your hands are one of the most sensitive parts of your body.
Packed with nerve endings, your fingertips can detect textures and temperatures with incredible precision.

Your gut contains more neurons than your spinal cord.
No wonder it's called the "second brain"—your gut's nervous system is vital for digestion and even influences mood.

Your body glows brighter in the afternoon.
Bioluminescence emitted by your body peaks during the late afternoon, likely due to metabolic activity.

You spend about 6 years of your life dreaming.
That's assuming an average of 2 hours of dreaming per night. If only we could remember more of those dreams!

Your lungs can hold about 6 liters of air.
With every breath, your lungs expand and contract to keep oxygen flowing and carbon dioxide exiting.

Your body replaces about 98% of its atoms annually.
Through a combination of metabolism, respiration, and other processes, almost all the atoms in your body are replaced each year.

You lose about a cup of water daily just by breathing.
Water vapor escapes with every exhale, contributing to your body's total water loss.

Your hair is stronger than copper wire.
Strand for strand, human hair can hold more weight than copper of the same thickness.

Your body contains about 37.5 trillion cells—and each one has its own job.
From red blood cells carrying oxygen to neurons firing signals, your cells are like a bustling city.

Your veins contain valves to prevent backflow.
These tiny flaps ensure that blood flows in the right direction, even against gravity.

Your fingernails grow faster than your toenails.
On average, fingernails grow about 3 millimeters per month, while toenails lag behind at 1 millimeter.

Your body creates about 300 billion new cells every day.
This constant regeneration ensures that damaged or old cells are replaced efficiently.

Your sense of touch can detect objects as small as 13 nanometers.
That's about 7,500 times smaller than the width of a human hair. Your fingertips are incredible sensors!

Your brain is about 73% water.
Dehydration by just 2% can impair your attention, memory, and cognitive skills. So, drink up—it's brain fuel.

Your small intestine is about 4 times your height.
Despite being coiled up inside you, the average small intestine stretches to about 22 feet in length, making it the ultimate overachiever.

You have about 2,000 taste buds on your tongue.
These tiny sensory organs help you experience the five basic tastes: sweet, sour, salty, bitter, and umami.

Your eyes blink in perfect synchronization.
Thanks to tiny muscles, your eyelids move in unison to protect and moisturize your eyes. Blink and you'll miss it—literally.

Your body contains about 0.2 milligrams of uranium.
While it sounds alarming, this naturally occurring element is found in trace amounts in the food and water we consume.

Your teeth start forming before you're born.
Even though they don't erupt until infancy, the foundations of your teeth begin forming as early as 6 weeks into fetal development.

Your brain can read up to 1,000 words per minute.
Under ideal conditions, your brain can process written text at an incredible speed—though comprehension might lag behind.

You can't swallow and breathe at the same time.
A special flap called the epiglottis closes off your windpipe when you swallow, ensuring food goes down the right way.

Your body temperature is slightly lower when you're lying down.
Gravity affects blood flow and metabolic processes, making you slightly cooler when resting horizontally.

Your fingerprints are formed in the womb.
The unique ridges on your fingertips develop between 13 and 19 weeks of pregnancy, influenced by movement and environmental factors in the womb.

Your ears are self-cleaning.
Earwax might seem gross, but it's your body's natural way of cleaning and protecting your ears from dirt and bacteria.

Your tongue has eight muscles.
Unlike most muscles, the tongue is not anchored to bone at both ends, giving it incredible flexibility and strength.

The cornea is the only part of the body with no blood supply.
It gets oxygen directly from the air, which is why contact lenses must allow oxygen to pass through to keep your eyes healthy.

Humans can make over 7,000 facial expressions.
Thanks to 43 muscles in the face, we're capable of expressing an astonishing range of emotions—from joy to confusion.

Your nails grow faster during pregnancy.
Hormonal changes and increased blood flow during pregnancy often speed up nail growth—a small silver lining for expectant mothers.

You can't see your own blind spot.
Everyone has a blind spot in their vision where the optic nerve connects to the retina, but your brain cleverly fills in the gap.

Your left lung is smaller than your right lung.
To make room for your heart, your left lung is slightly smaller and has two lobes instead of three.

Your brain has more connections than stars in the Milky Way.
With an estimated 100 trillion neural connections, your brain is the most complex known structure in the universe.

The human body glows more brightly at night.
Though invisible to the naked eye, your body emits slightly more bioluminescent light during the late evening hours due to metabolic processes.

You breathe about 20,000 times a day.
Each breath brings oxygen to your bloodstream and removes carbon dioxide, keeping your body alive and functioning.

The pink part of your fingernail is called the lunula.
This crescent-shaped area is a sign of healthy nails and is most visible on the thumbs.

SPACE AND THE UNIVERSE

Facts that explore the cosmos and our place in it.

The Sun accounts for 99.86% of the mass in the Solar System.
Everything else—planets, moons, asteroids, and comets—makes up the remaining 0.14%. The Sun is literally the heavyweight champion of our cosmic neighborhood.

A day on Venus is longer than a year.
Venus takes 243 Earth days to rotate once on its axis but only 225 Earth days to orbit the Sun. Imagine celebrating your birthday before the day is over.

Neutron stars are so dense that a sugar-cube-sized piece would weigh a billion tons.
If you could somehow hold a piece of a neutron star, it would weigh as much as a mountain. Good luck picking it up.

There's a giant cloud of alcohol floating in space.
Located near the constellation Sagittarius, this interstellar cloud contains enough ethyl alcohol to produce 400 trillion pints of beer. Too bad it's 58 quadrillion miles away.

One spoonful of a black hole would weigh as much as the entire Earth.
Black holes are so dense that their mass is packed into an incredibly small space, creating gravity so strong not even light can escape.

There's a planet made entirely of diamonds.
55 Cancri e, a planet twice the size of Earth, is believed to have a diamond-rich core. It's the ultimate bling in the cosmos.

Space smells like burnt steak.
Astronauts returning from spacewalks have described a peculiar smell on their suits, similar to seared meat or welding fumes.

The Moon is moving away from Earth.
Every year, the Moon drifts about 1.5 inches farther from Earth. In about 50 billion years, it'll be too far away to cause solar eclipses.

Jupiter's Great Red Spot is shrinking.
This iconic storm has been raging for over 350 years but is gradually getting smaller. It's still big enough to fit three Earths inside, though.

The largest volcano in the Solar System is on Mars.
Olympus Mons stands about 13.6 miles high, nearly three times the height of Mount Everest. Mars clearly likes to overachieve.

Saturn's moon Titan has a weather system like Earth's—except it rains methane.
Methane cycles through Titan's atmosphere, forming lakes and rivers of liquid natural gas. Don't forget your heatproof umbrella.

A day on Mars lasts 24 hours and 39 minutes.
If you ever move to Mars, you'd only need to slightly tweak your schedule to adapt to Martian time.

The universe is expanding faster than the speed of light.
While nothing within the universe can travel faster than light, the space between galaxies is stretching at a speed that exceeds this limit.

A star is born every 10 seconds.
In galaxies across the universe, new stars are constantly forming, ensuring that the night sky never runs out of sparkle.

There are more stars in the universe than grains of sand on Earth.
The observable universe contains roughly 1 sextillion stars—an unfathomable number that dwarfs every beach and desert combined.

Venus is the hottest planet in the Solar System.
Despite being farther from the Sun, Venus's thick atmosphere traps heat through a runaway greenhouse effect, reaching temperatures of 900°F.

There's a rogue planet hurtling through space.
Known as a "rogue planet," PSO J318.5-22 drifts through space without orbiting a star. It's essentially a cosmic wanderer.

The Milky Way and Andromeda galaxies are on a collision course.
In about 4.5 billion years, our galaxy will merge with Andromeda, creating a new galactic mega-structure. Don't worry, Earth will survive—probably.

The surface area of Pluto is smaller than Russia.
Despite its planetary controversy, Pluto's total surface area is only about 16.7 million square kilometers, making it smaller than Earth's largest country.

A year on Mercury is just 88 days long.
Mercury orbits the Sun at breakneck speed, completing a year in less than three Earth months.

There are "cold spots" in space.
The coldest natural place in the universe is the Boomerang Nebula, where temperatures drop to minus 457.6°F, colder than the cosmic microwave background.

Black holes can "spit out" material.
Though known for pulling everything in, some black holes emit jets of energy and particles at nearly the speed of light, creating spectacular cosmic shows.

The Solar System travels at 514,000 mph around the Milky Way.
Earth isn't just spinning—it's also hurtling through space as our entire Solar System orbits the galactic center.

Mars has the tallest canyon in the Solar System.
Valles Marineris stretches 2,500 miles long and is up to 7 miles deep. It makes the Grand Canyon look like a tiny crack in the ground.

The Sun will eventually become a white dwarf.
In about 5 billion years, the Sun will exhaust its fuel, expand into a red giant, and then shrink into a white dwarf—a stellar retirement plan.

The Moon causes Earth's tides.
The gravitational pull of the Moon creates bulges in Earth's oceans, leading to the high and low tides we experience daily.

A year on Uranus lasts 84 Earth years.
Uranus takes so long to orbit the Sun that one year on the planet would span an entire human lifetime.

The Sun is middle-aged.
At about 4.6 billion years old, the Sun is roughly halfway through its life cycle. It has another 5 billion years before it runs out of fuel and becomes a white dwarf.

The Kuiper Belt is like the Solar System's junkyard.
This region beyond Neptune is filled with icy bodies, dwarf planets, and debris left over from the formation of the Solar System.

There's a "super-Earth" where it rains molten glass sideways.
HD 189733b, an exoplanet 63 light-years away, experiences glass rain driven by winds of up to 5,400 mph.

A day on Uranus lasts 17 hours and 14 minutes.
Its rapid rotation and extreme axial tilt make Uranus one of the most peculiar planets in the Solar System.

The Hubble Space Telescope has traveled over 4 billion miles.
Since its launch in 1990, Hubble has orbited Earth more than 190,000 times, capturing breathtaking images of the universe.

You could fit 1.3 million Earths inside the Sun.
The Sun's volume is so massive that over a million Earths could fit within it, highlighting its incredible scale.

Mars has seasons like Earth.
Because of its tilted axis, Mars experiences seasons similar to ours, though they last nearly twice as long due to its longer orbit.

Pluto's orbit is shaped like a squashed oval.
Unlike the circular orbits of most planets, Pluto's elliptical orbit occasionally brings it closer to the Sun than Neptune.

The universe is 13.8 billion years old.
Scientists estimate the age of the universe based on the cosmic microwave background radiation, a faint glow left over from the Big Bang.

Earth's magnetic field shields us from solar winds.
The magnetosphere deflects charged particles from the Sun, preventing them from stripping away our atmosphere.

There's a hexagon-shaped storm on Saturn.
The planet's north pole features a massive, long-lasting storm shaped like a perfect hexagon, baffling scientists.

The Milky Way smells like rum and tastes like raspberries.
The center of our galaxy contains ethyl formate, a chemical responsible for the flavor of raspberries and the smell of rum.

Earth has a "second moon."
Asteroid 3753 Cruithne orbits the Sun in a synchronized pattern with Earth, earning it the nickname "Earth's second moon."

It rains diamonds on Saturn and Jupiter.
High pressures in their atmospheres can compress carbon into diamond rain—a literal cosmic treasure.

The hottest planet in the Solar System isn't closest to the Sun.
Venus, not Mercury, holds the title due to its dense atmosphere trapping heat through an extreme greenhouse effect.

The Milky Way is on a diet.
Our galaxy is slowly "eating" smaller satellite galaxies like the Sagittarius Dwarf Galaxy, merging their stars into its structure.

A teaspoon of neutron star material would weigh 10 million tons.
Neutron stars are so dense that a tiny piece of one would outweigh some of Earth's largest structures.

Saturn's rings are younger than the dinosaurs.
While the planet is billions of years old, its iconic rings likely formed just 100–200 million years ago.

The dark side of the Moon isn't always dark.
The Moon rotates, so every part of it gets sunlight. "Dark side" just means the side that's permanently facing away from Earth.

A day on the Moon lasts about 29 Earth days.
Because the Moon rotates so slowly, its day is nearly as long as an entire lunar month.

Stars don't twinkle in space.
The twinkling effect is caused by Earth's atmosphere. In space, stars shine steadily.

There are potentially more universes than stars.
The multiverse theory suggests that our universe might be just one of countless others, each with its own laws of physics.

The first exoplanet was discovered in 1992.
Since then, thousands of exoplanets have been identified, many of which could potentially host life.

The Moon has "moonquakes."
Like earthquakes, moonquakes occur due to tidal forces and the cooling of the Moon's interior.

Mars is home to the largest dust storms in the Solar System.
These storms can cover the entire planet and last for months, making Mars a dusty nightmare.

The speed of light is the ultimate speed limit.
At 186,282 miles per second, nothing in the universe can travel faster than light—except, perhaps, the expansion of the universe itself.

The Sun's core is 27 million degrees Fahrenheit.
This staggering temperature is the result of nuclear fusion, the process powering our star.

Earth is the densest planet in the Solar System.
Despite being smaller than gas giants, Earth's rocky composition makes it the densest planet.

The Solar System has an edge.
The heliopause, where the Sun's influence ends and interstellar space begins, marks the boundary of our Solar System.

There's a "great wall" of galaxies.
The Hercules-Corona Borealis Great Wall is a massive galaxy supercluster spanning 10 billion light-years.

The Moon was once part of Earth.
The leading theory suggests the Moon formed after a Mars-sized object collided with Earth billions of years ago.

Neptune's winds can reach 1,200 mph.
These supersonic winds make Neptune the windiest planet in the Solar System.

Mercury has virtually no atmosphere.
Without a substantial atmosphere, Mercury experiences temperature swings of over 1,000°F between day and night.

The Andromeda Galaxy is twice the size of the Milky Way.
Andromeda contains about a trillion stars compared to the Milky Way's estimated 200–400 billion.

The Sun is technically white.
Although it appears yellow from Earth, the Sun emits light across all wavelengths, making it white in space.

A day on Earth used to last just 6 hours.
Billions of years ago, Earth spun much faster, resulting in much shorter days.

The largest asteroid is almost a dwarf planet.
Ceres, the largest asteroid in the asteroid belt, is so massive it's classified as a dwarf planet.

There's a star that's cooler than the human body.
Some brown dwarfs have surface temperatures as low as 80°F, making them cooler than you on a summer day.

There's a black hole 6 billion times the mass of the Sun.
The supermassive black hole in the galaxy M87 has been imaged by scientists and is unimaginably massive.

Astronauts' heights increase in space.
In microgravity, the spine stretches, making astronauts up to 2 inches taller during their time in orbit.

The Earth's shadow causes lunar eclipses.
When Earth comes between the Sun and the Moon, its shadow darkens the Moon, creating a spectacular celestial event.

There's a volcano on Venus that might still be active.
Recent studies suggest some of Venus's volcanoes could still be erupting, reshaping the planet's surface.

Earth is the only planet not named after a god.
Every other planet in the Solar System is named after Roman or Greek deities, while Earth's name comes from Old English and Germanic roots.

A neutron star can spin 600 times per second.
These ultra-dense remnants of supernovae rotate at incredible speeds, creating pulsars that emit beams of radiation.

There are more molecules in a glass of water than stars in the universe.
A single glass of water contains about 10^{25} molecules, far exceeding the estimated number of stars in the observable universe.

The coldest place in the universe is on Earth.
Scientists at MIT created a lab experiment where temperatures reached 100 trillionths of a degree above absolute zero.

Venus spins backward.
Unlike most planets, Venus rotates in the opposite direction of its orbit around the Sun.

One year on Neptune lasts 165 Earth years.
Neptune's distant orbit makes it the slowest planet to complete a trip around the Sun.

Earth's axis is tilted at 23.5 degrees.
This tilt is responsible for the changing seasons as the planet orbits the Sun.

The Sun's energy could power Earth for 500,000 years in one second.
Every second, the Sun produces enough energy to meet all of Earth's needs for half a million years.

Mars has two moons—Phobos and Deimos.
These irregularly shaped moons are thought to be captured asteroids from the asteroid belt.

A black hole can "evaporate."
Through Hawking radiation, black holes slowly lose mass and energy over time, potentially disappearing entirely.

The Milky Way is a barred spiral galaxy.
Our galaxy has a central bar structure made of stars, distinguishing it from a traditional spiral galaxy.

Jupiter's magnetic field is 20,000 times stronger than Earth's.
This massive magnetic field creates intense radiation belts and spectacular auroras on the gas giant.

The universe could end in a "big freeze."
If expansion continues indefinitely, galaxies will drift apart, and the universe could cool to near absolute zero.

The Moon's gravity causes Earth's rotation to slow.
Tidal interactions between Earth and the Moon are gradually increasing the length of our days by about 1.8 milliseconds per century.

Mercury has ice at its poles.
Despite being the closest planet to the Sun, Mercury's polar craters contain water ice, shielded from sunlight.

The International Space Station (ISS) travels at 17,500 mph.
Orbiting Earth every 90 minutes, astronauts on the ISS experience 16 sunrises and sunsets daily.

The largest moon in the Solar System is Ganymede.
Jupiter's moon Ganymede is even larger than the planet Mercury and has its own magnetic field.

The Big Bang wasn't an explosion.
It was the rapid expansion of space itself, creating the universe as we know it about 13.8 billion years ago.

Earth has "space quakes."
Similar to earthquakes, space quakes are caused by the interaction of solar winds with Earth's magnetosphere.

You weigh less on the Moon.
Due to its weaker gravity, you'd weigh only about 16.5% of your Earth weight on the Moon.

The Sun's atmosphere is hotter than its surface.
The corona, or outer layer, reaches temperatures of up to 3.5 million degrees Fahrenheit—much hotter than the Sun's surface.

Asteroids have moons.
Some large asteroids, like Ida, have smaller objects orbiting them, acting as moons.

A galaxy can have more than one black hole.
Many galaxies, including the Milky Way, host multiple black holes of various sizes, with a supermassive one at the center.

The Solar System formed from a giant molecular cloud.
About 4.6 billion years ago, a collapsing cloud of gas and dust gave birth to the Sun, planets, and other celestial bodies.

Jupiter has the shortest day in the Solar System.
The gas giant rotates once every 9 hours and 56 minutes, making its days incredibly short despite its size.

There are free-floating planets in space.
Rogue planets drift through interstellar space without being bound to any star.

The universe has a "cosmic web."
Galaxies and clusters are connected by massive filaments of dark matter, forming a web-like structure.

Saturn could float in water.
With its low density, Saturn would theoretically float if you could find a bathtub big enough.

Stars can "sing."
The vibrations in stars produce sound waves, creating oscillations that scientists study to learn about their internal structure.

Comets are leftovers from the Solar System's formation.
These icy objects are remnants of the early Solar System, preserved in deep freeze.

Mars has a canyon 10 times the size of the Grand Canyon.
Valles Marineris is so vast it would stretch across the entire United States.

The Moon has no atmosphere.
Without an atmosphere, the Moon has no weather, sound, or protection from meteors.

The Sun will eventually engulf Earth.
When it becomes a red giant in about 5 billion years, the Sun will expand and likely consume the inner planets.

There are planets where it rains iron.
On WASP-76b, temperatures are so extreme that vaporized iron condenses and falls as rain.

The Andromeda Galaxy contains 1 trillion stars.
Our neighboring galaxy is about twice the size of the Milky Way and is on a collision course with us.

The largest moon of Saturn, Titan, has an atmosphere thicker than Earth's.
Titan's dense atmosphere and liquid methane lakes make it one of the most Earth-like bodies in the Solar System.

Earth is traveling through space at 67,000 mph.
As Earth orbits the Sun, it hurtles through space at incredible speeds.

Pluto has a heart-shaped glacier.
The "heart" of Pluto, named Tombaugh Regio, is a massive glacier made of nitrogen ice.

Supernovae create elements.
Heavy elements like gold and uranium are forged in the intense explosions of dying stars.

There are 100 billion galaxies in the observable universe.
Each galaxy contains billions of stars, making the universe incomprehensibly vast.

The universe is flat.
Measurements show that on a large scale, the universe has a flat geometry, meaning parallel lines would never meet.

SCIENCE THAT SOUNDS LIKE SCI-FI

Strange discoveries and experiments in physics, chemistry, and biology.

There's a lab-grown brain that plays video games.
Scientists created a "mini-brain" from human neurons that can learn to play the game *Pong*. It's not just sci-fi—it's a glimpse into the future of artificial intelligence.

CERN's Large Hadron Collider can recreate the Big Bang.
This massive particle accelerator smashes atoms together at near-light speeds, mimicking conditions from the universe's birth.

You can turn air into diamonds.
By capturing carbon dioxide from the atmosphere and compressing it under high heat and pressure, scientists can create diamonds—a truly futuristic recycling project.

CRISPR lets us edit DNA like a word processor.
This revolutionary technology allows scientists to "cut and paste" genetic material, potentially curing diseases or even designing babies.

We can grow human organs in pigs.
Using gene-editing technology, scientists have grown human-compatible organs in pigs, offering hope for transplant patients.

There's a material that's lighter than air and 10 times stronger than steel.
Aerographene, a form of graphene, is so lightweight it can rest on a flower petal while being incredibly strong. It's like something out of a superhero movie.

Scientists have figured out how to teleport particles.
Quantum entanglement allows particles to transmit information instantaneously across vast distances. It's not Star Trek-level teleportation yet, but it's close.

We've created "invisibility cloaks."
Using metamaterials, researchers have developed cloaks that bend light around objects, rendering them invisible—just like Harry Potter's cloak.

There's a laser that's brighter than 1,000 suns.
The Extreme Light Infrastructure laser produces bursts of light so intense they can create matter from empty space, challenging our understanding of physics.

We can send data faster than the speed of light.
Using quantum tunneling, information can bypass the speed-of-light limit—at least in theoretical setups. It's Einstein-approved sci-fi.

Artificial skin can feel.
Engineers have developed synthetic skin that mimics human touch, complete with sensors for temperature, pressure, and pain.

You can grow meat in a lab.
Lab-grown meat, created from animal cells, doesn't require slaughtering animals and could revolutionize food production.

We've created a real-life "tractor beam."
Using sound waves, scientists have developed a way to levitate and move small objects, much like the tractor beams in sci-fi movies.

We've detected "zombie" stars.
White dwarf stars can reignite by stealing material from nearby stars, creating a second, brief life in the cosmos.

3D printers can build houses.
Massive 3D printers are capable of constructing entire homes in under 24 hours, potentially solving housing crises in the future.

There are robots made of living cells.
Xenobots, made from frog cells, can move, heal themselves, and even reproduce—a fusion of biology and robotics straight out of *Blade Runner*.

Scientists have made mice glow in the dark.
By inserting jellyfish DNA into mice, researchers created glowing rodents—an experiment that could one day help visualize diseases.

You can store data in DNA.
A single gram of DNA can store 215 petabytes of data, making it the ultimate compact storage device for the future.

We've developed self-healing materials.
Materials that can repair themselves when damaged, inspired by human skin, are already being tested for use in construction and electronics.

There's a "water tractor beam."
Scientists have created a way to move water against gravity using sound waves, defying conventional physics.

Time crystals exist.
These bizarre phases of matter change their structure over time without using energy, defying the laws of thermodynamics.

We can make robots sweat.
Researchers developed robots with pores that release water to cool down, mimicking human perspiration for improved performance.

Quantum computers can solve problems classical computers can't.
These next-generation machines use quantum bits to perform calculations at speeds that make regular computers look ancient.

Scientists can print human tissue.
3D bioprinters are capable of creating living tissues and even organs, paving the way for personalized medicine and transplants.

We've created "antimatter."
The counterpart to matter, antimatter is so rare and powerful that just one gram could power a city for days.

We can control machines with our thoughts.
Brain-computer interfaces allow people to operate devices like prosthetic limbs and drones using only their minds.

There's a substance that gets colder when you heat it.
Vanadium dioxide, a strange material, behaves counterintuitively, cooling down when heated under certain conditions.

We've sent robots to the bottom of the ocean.
Autonomous submersibles have explored the Mariana Trench, the deepest part of Earth's oceans, where pressures would crush most machines.

Fusion reactors could power the future.
Scientists are working on harnessing nuclear fusion, the same process that powers the Sun, for nearly limitless clean energy.

We can extract oxygen from moon dust.
A process developed for future lunar missions could turn moon dust into breathable oxygen, bringing us one step closer to colonizing the Moon.

We've "frozen" light.
Researchers have slowed light to a near standstill in lab experiments, challenging our understanding of its speed.

Artificial intelligence can compose symphonies.
AI programs like AIVA have created original music, rivaling compositions by human musicians.

We can reverse aging in cells.
Experiments with cellular reprogramming have shown promise in reversing the aging process, at least in mice.

There's a laser that can write in the air.
By ionizing particles in the atmosphere, lasers can create glowing, free-floating 3D images in mid-air.

We've built computers smaller than a grain of rice.
These microcomputers, used for medical and environmental monitoring, are so tiny they could revolutionize technology.

There's a "synthetic leaf" that turns sunlight into fuel.
Inspired by photosynthesis, scientists have developed devices that convert solar energy into usable fuels like hydrogen.

We've discovered a new state of matter.
Bose-Einstein condensates are ultra-cold states of matter where particles behave as a single quantum entity, rewriting the rulebook of physics.

You can buy clothes made of spider silk.
Synthetic spider silk, stronger than steel and incredibly lightweight, is being used to make high-tech fabrics.

We can read people's thoughts.
Using brain-scanning technology and AI, researchers can interpret brain activity to reconstruct words, images, and even dreams.

There are pills that can turn your sweat pink.
Researchers have developed capsules that contain compounds which change the color of your sweat, designed for monitoring hydration levels.

We've created bionic eyes.
Prosthetic eyes with cameras and sensors can restore partial sight to blind individuals—a breakthrough that feels like it's straight out of *The Terminator*.

Scientists have teleported information to space.
Quantum entanglement experiments have successfully transmitted information between Earth and satellites, paving the way for quantum communication.

We've engineered plants to glow.
Using genes from bioluminescent organisms, scientists have created glowing plants that could one day replace streetlights.

We can grow "mini-organs" in labs.
Organoids, small-scale versions of human organs, are being used to study diseases and test new treatments.

There are self-driving drones that deliver organs.
Drones equipped with advanced navigation systems are now used to transport human organs for transplants, saving precious time.

You can buy self-cleaning clothes.
Clothes treated with nanotechnology can repel dirt and bacteria, staying clean even after weeks of wear without washing.

Scientists are creating artificial gravity.
Experiments on rotating spacecraft and centrifuges aim to simulate Earth-like gravity for astronauts in space.

We can "print" entire buildings.
3D printers capable of constructing multi-story buildings are already being tested, promising cheaper and faster housing solutions.

There's a machine that turns air into water.
Atmospheric water generators extract moisture from the air, providing clean drinking water in arid regions.

We've developed a vaccine for cancer.
Personalized cancer vaccines that train the immune system to attack tumors are showing promise in clinical trials.

There's a robot surgeon.
Robotic systems like the da Vinci Surgical System perform precise, minimally invasive surgeries with incredible accuracy.

We can "harvest" electricity from the air.
Using materials that absorb atmospheric moisture, scientists have developed devices that generate small amounts of electricity.

There's a computer powered by water droplets.
This experimental computer uses tiny droplets of water as data bits, combining fluid mechanics with computation.

We can create artificial stars.
Fusion reactors like ITER aim to replicate the process of stellar energy production here on Earth.

Scientists have built a time crystal.
Time crystals are a new phase of matter that repeat their structure in time rather than space, defying conventional physics.

You can charge your phone with your body heat.
Thermoelectric devices convert body heat into electricity, offering a futuristic way to power gadgets.

We've created "smart tattoos."
Temporary tattoos embedded with electronic sensors can monitor health metrics like heart rate and hydration.

There's a car that runs on saltwater.
The Quant e-Sportlimousine uses a flow cell battery that converts saltwater into electricity, achieving speeds of up to 217 mph.

We've synthesized living cells.
Scientists created the first artificial cell with a synthetic genome, marking a milestone in synthetic biology.

You can "erase" traumatic memories.
Researchers are exploring ways to block or modify memory formation, offering potential treatments for PTSD.

There's a lab that mimics a black hole.
Using ultra-cold atoms, scientists have created an Earth-bound black hole analog to study its properties.

We've cloned animals from cells frozen for decades.
Japanese scientists cloned mice using cells that had been frozen for 16 years, pushing the boundaries of cloning technology.

We can communicate with plants.
Using bio-electrochemical sensors, scientists can detect electrical signals in plants, essentially "talking" to them about their health.

We can use sound to levitate objects.
Acoustic levitation uses sound waves to suspend small objects in mid-air, with potential applications in manufacturing and medicine.

There's a camera that can see around corners.
Advanced imaging systems use reflected light to create images of objects hidden from direct view.

We've made water boil without heat.
Using a process called cavitation, scientists can create bubbles that cause water to boil through pressure alone.

You can charge your phone with sound.
Sound energy harvesters convert ambient noise into electricity, offering a new way to power devices.

We've discovered a "fifth force" of nature.
Beyond gravity, electromagnetism, and nuclear forces, physicists suspect a new force influencing subatomic particles.

Artificial neurons can replace damaged ones.
Lab-made neurons can mimic the function of biological ones, potentially treating conditions like Parkinson's and Alzheimer's.

We've developed robots that repair themselves.
Soft robots made of self-healing materials can fix their own damage, extending their usability in harsh environments.

There's a spray-on solar panel.
Scientists have developed a sprayable photovoltaic material that can turn any surface into a solar energy collector.

We can grow coral in labs to save reefs.
Artificial reefs made from lab-grown coral are helping restore marine ecosystems affected by climate change.

We've developed computers that learn on their own.
AI systems like neural networks can now teach themselves new skills, mimicking human learning processes.

There's a suit that lets you breathe underwater.
Experimental designs using artificial gills extract oxygen from water, allowing divers to stay submerged without tanks.

We've created robots that evolve.
Using algorithms, robots can "mutate" their design and functions over time to adapt to new challenges.

Scientists are creating "living concrete."
Concrete embedded with bacteria can heal its own cracks, reducing the need for maintenance in buildings and roads.

We can 3D-print bones.
Medical-grade 3D printers can create custom bone replacements using biocompatible materials.

We've detected the "voice" of atoms.
Using ultra-sensitive instruments, scientists have measured the vibrations of individual atoms, essentially listening to their "sound."

There are clothes that regulate your temperature.
Smart fabrics embedded with sensors can heat or cool your body based on environmental conditions.

We've created synthetic blood.
Lab-made blood is being developed to address shortages and save lives in emergencies.

There's a material that absorbs 99.995% of light.
Vantablack, the darkest material ever created, makes objects appear completely flat and featureless.

We've created holograms you can touch.
Using ultrasound waves, researchers have developed holograms that give the sensation of touch, bringing sci-fi displays closer to reality.

You can regrow teeth with lasers.
Scientists have discovered that low-power laser beams can stimulate stem cells to regenerate dentin, the material in teeth.

We can "print" food.
3D food printers use edible materials to create intricate meals, making futuristic kitchens a present-day reality.

There are robots that can reproduce.
Xenobots, made from frog cells, have demonstrated the ability to replicate themselves under specific conditions.

We've developed clothing that repairs itself.
Textiles made with self-healing polymers can mend small tears when exposed to heat or pressure.

There's a machine that creates fuel from sunlight.
Solar-to-fuel reactors mimic photosynthesis to produce hydrogen and other fuels from sunlight, water, and CO2.

We've created "programmable water."
Scientists have engineered water droplets that can act as tiny robots, performing tasks like transporting materials.

You can grow plants in lunar soil.
NASA experiments have successfully grown crops using simulated Moon soil, paving the way for space farming.

We've built "soft robots" that mimic human muscles.
Soft robotic systems replicate the flexibility and strength of natural muscles for use in prosthetics and automation.

There are windows that turn into solar panels.
Smart windows embedded with transparent photovoltaic cells can generate electricity while letting in light.

We've created a spray that turns surfaces into touchscreens.
This conductive spray allows any flat surface to function as a touchscreen interface.

We can "print" entire human bones.
3D-printed bones made from biomaterials are being used to replace damaged or missing skeletal parts in patients.

There's a device that turns seawater into drinkable water in minutes.
Using advanced filtration, portable desalination units can provide clean drinking water from the ocean.

We've developed clothing that changes color.
Smart fabrics embedded with nanotechnology can alter their color and pattern based on heat or light.

You can control a drone with your mind.
Brain-computer interfaces allow users to pilot drones using just their thoughts, no hands required.

We've created invisibility shields for sound.
Acoustic metamaterials can redirect sound waves, creating "invisible" zones for noise reduction.

There's a robot that can dissolve itself after completing its task.
Disposable robots made from biodegradable materials can self-destruct after use, reducing waste.

We've engineered plants to remove toxic chemicals from the air.
Genetically modified houseplants can clean indoor air by absorbing harmful compounds more efficiently than natural plants.

There are "living tattoos" made from bacteria.
These bioengineered tattoos can sense environmental changes like pollution or temperature and respond visibly.

We've created a gel that can stop bleeding in seconds.
Hemostatic gels rapidly seal wounds, saving lives in emergencies by preventing blood loss.

There's a pill that can mimic exercise.
Experimental drugs stimulate the effects of exercise on muscles, potentially benefiting people unable to work out.

We've created clothing that generates electricity.
Wearable fabrics embedded with piezoelectric materials can convert movement into small amounts of power.

You can "farm" electricity from algae.
Bio-energy systems use photosynthetic algae to generate electricity while absorbing CO_2.

We've made plants that glow brighter than streetlights.
Using nanoparticles, researchers have created plants with intense bioluminescence for sustainable lighting.

POP CULTURE MARVELS

Fun and shocking facts about movies, music, and celebrities.

The first music video played on MTV was "Video Killed the Radio Star."
This iconic track by The Buggles kicked off MTV's launch on August 1, 1981, forever changing the music industry.

The voice of Darth Vader and Mufasa is the same person.
James Earl Jones lent his deep, commanding voice to both iconic characters, making him a pop culture legend.

Michael Jackson tried to buy Marvel Comics.
In the late 1990s, Jackson considered buying Marvel so he could play Spider-Man in a movie. Unfortunately (or fortunately), it didn't happen.

The Simpsons is the longest-running American sitcom.
Since debuting in 1989, *The Simpsons* has aired over 700 episodes, cementing its place in television history.

The first ever YouTube video was about elephants.
Titled *Me at the zoo*, the 19-second clip features co-founder Jawed Karim talking about elephants at the San Diego Zoo.

The Beatles once had a cartoon show.
From 1965 to 1969, an animated series featured caricatured versions of the Fab Four, introducing them to younger audiences.

Stan Lee made cameos in over 30 Marvel films.
The legendary comic book creator appeared in almost every Marvel Cinematic Universe movie before his passing in 2018.

The highest-grossing movie of all time is *Avatar*. (so far)
James Cameron's sci-fi epic reclaimed the title in 2021, surpassing *Avengers: Endgame* with a worldwide gross of over $2.9 billion.

Elvis Presley had a black belt in karate.
The King of Rock and Roll was a skilled martial artist and even incorporated karate moves into his stage performances.

The Harry Potter books were rejected 12 times.
J.K. Rowling's manuscript was turned down by numerous publishers before Bloomsbury took a chance, launching one of the biggest franchises ever.

Walt Disney was afraid of mice.
Ironically, the creator of Mickey Mouse reportedly had a fear of rodents in real life.

Keanu Reeves gave away most of his *The Matrix* earnings.
Reeves donated approximately $75 million to the film's special effects and makeup teams, proving he's as generous as he is talented.

The Monopoly game board is based on Atlantic City.
The famous properties—Boardwalk, Park Place, and others—are named after real streets in the New Jersey city.

The *Friends* cast negotiated equal pay as a group.
By the end of the series, all six main actors were earning $1 million per episode, thanks to their solidarity during contract negotiations.

The character of Dracula has appeared in over 200 films.
Bram Stoker's infamous vampire holds the record as the most portrayed character in film history.

Madonna holds the record for the highest-grossing female concert tour.
Her *Sticky & Sweet Tour* in 2008–2009 grossed over $408 million, setting a benchmark for female artists.

Pac-Man was inspired by pizza.
The design of the iconic arcade character was modeled after a pizza with a slice missing, symbolizing endless munching.

Marvel almost went bankrupt in the 1990s.
The company's financial struggles led to the sale of character rights like Spider-Man to Sony and X-Men to Fox, shaping the MCU's early challenges.

The voice of Shrek was originally Chris Farley.
Farley recorded most of Shrek's dialogue before his untimely death. Mike Myers later took over, transforming the character's personality and accent.

The "E.T. finger" used to glow with a real medical tool.
The iconic glowing effect in *E.T.* was achieved using a real-life medical device used to check oxygen levels in patients.

The Tetris theme song is a Russian folk tune.
The catchy music, known as *Korobeiniki*, is a 19th-century Russian folk song about a traveling merchant.

Tom Cruise performs his own stunts.
From scaling skyscrapers to jumping out of planes, Cruise insists on doing his own stunts in movies like *Mission: Impossible*.

Oprah Winfrey's production company is called Harpo.
"Harpo" is Oprah spelled backward, a creative nod to her name and her business acumen.

The character of Sherlock Holmes has appeared in over 250 films.
The great detective holds the Guinness World Record for the most portrayed literary character in film and television.

The *Star Wars* lightsaber sound was made with a TV and a projector motor.
Sound designer Ben Burtt created the iconic hum by blending the buzz of an old TV with the motor of a 16mm projector.

There's a *Toy Story* Easter egg in every Pixar film.
A reference to the Pizza Planet truck or another nod to *Toy Story* appears in every movie from Pixar's catalog.

The most-streamed song of all time is by The Weeknd.
As of now, "Blinding Lights" holds the record for the most streams on Spotify, redefining pop music in the streaming era.

The first-ever tweet was "just setting up my twttr."
Posted by Jack Dorsey in 2006, this unassuming tweet launched the platform that changed how we communicate.

The Batmobile in *Batman Begins* was real and functional.
The "Tumbler" was a fully operational vehicle capable of high-speed chases and impressive stunts.

The longest-running comic strip is *The Katzenjammer Kids*.
First published in 1897, this strip holds the record for the longest continuous publication in comic strip history.

The *Friends* couch is still in Warner Bros. Studio.
The orange couch from Central Perk is a popular attraction for fans visiting the studio's backlot tour.

James Bond has worn over 30 Rolex watches in the movies.
Bond's preference for luxury watches has made brands like Rolex and Omega iconic in pop culture.

The *Game of Thrones* finale was watched by over 19 million people.
Despite its controversial ending, the series finale set viewership records for HBO.

Michael Jordan's "Space Jam" jersey sold for $320,000.
The *Space Jam* memorabilia became one of the most expensive sports movie props ever sold at auction.

The Disney castle logo was inspired by Neuschwanstein Castle in Germany.
Walt Disney modeled the iconic symbol after the fairytale-like castle in Bavaria.

Leonardo da Vinci's *Mona Lisa* was once stolen.
In 1911, the famous painting was taken from the Louvre and recovered two years later, cementing its global fame.

The Marvel Cinematic Universe is the highest-grossing movie franchise.
With over $29 billion in global earnings, the MCU dominates the box office record books.

The name "Lego" comes from Danish words meaning "play well."
It's derived from *leg godt*, perfectly capturing the spirit of the world's most popular building toy.

The *Cheers* bar is based on a real place in Boston.
The Bull & Finch Pub inspired the setting of the hit TV show, and it remains a tourist hotspot.

There's a hidden Mickey in almost every Disney movie.
Disney animators sneak the iconic mouse silhouette into their films, challenging fans to find them all.

The voice of Mickey Mouse was Walt Disney himself.
Walt provided Mickey's voice from his creation in 1928 until 1947, personally giving life to the beloved character.

The original *Jurassic Park* T. rex roar was a mix of animal sounds.
Sound designers blended recordings of a baby elephant, an alligator, and a tiger to create the iconic roar.

The Hollywood sign originally read "Hollywoodland."
Erected in 1923 as an advertisement for a real estate development, the "land" was dropped in 1949.

Marvel's Spider-Man was almost a fly.
Stan Lee initially considered creating a superhero called Fly-Man but decided Spider-Man sounded cooler—and he was right.

The longest-running talk show host was Johnny Carson.
Carson hosted *The Tonight Show* for 30 years, from 1962 to 1992, setting the standard for late-night TV.

The first superhero was The Phantom.
Debuting in 1936, The Phantom predates Superman and Batman, marking the beginning of the superhero genre.

***The Wizard of Oz* slippers were originally silver.**
In L. Frank Baum's book, Dorothy's shoes were silver, but the movie changed them to ruby to showcase Technicolor.

Netflix was founded as a DVD rental service.
The streaming giant started in 1997 by mailing DVDs to customers before revolutionizing on-demand content.

The *Friends* theme song was almost a different song.
Producers originally wanted *Shiny Happy People* by R.E.M., but the band declined, paving the way for *I'll Be There for You* by The Rembrandts.

The first animated feature film was not Disney's.
Disney's *Snow White* is often credited, but *El Apóstol* (1917) from Argentina holds the true title, though its reels were lost in a fire.

There are over 12,000 unique items in the *Star Wars* archives.
From costumes to props, Lucasfilm's collection spans decades of filmmaking and lore-building.

Mr. Rogers was colorblind.
Fred Rogers, the beloved children's television host, was red-green colorblind, though it never impacted his love for colorful sweaters.

The word "robot" comes from a Czech play.
The term was coined in Karel Čapek's 1920 play *R.U.R. (Rossum's Universal Robots)*, derived from the Czech word *robota*, meaning forced labor.

The shortest Oscar speech was just two words.
When Alfred Hitchcock received his Irving G. Thalberg Memorial Award in 1968, he simply said, "Thank you."

The Beatles hold the record for the most No. 1 hits on the Billboard charts.
With 20 chart-toppers, the Fab Four remain the reigning kings of pop music success.

Super Mario was named after a landlord.
Mario Segale, the landlord of Nintendo's American offices, inspired the name of the iconic video game character.

The most expensive movie ever made is *Pirates of the Caribbean: On Stranger Tides*.
With a budget of $379 million, the fourth *Pirates* film tops the list of costly productions.

The first TV commercial aired in 1941.
A 10-second ad for Bulova watches aired during a baseball game, costing just $9.

The most-watched television broadcast was the moon landing.
An estimated 650 million people watched Neil Armstrong take humanity's first steps on the Moon in 1969.

There's a Marvel superhero inspired by Elvis Presley.
The character Dazzler, who can turn sound into light, was partly inspired by The King's flashy persona.

The first product ever sold on eBay was a broken laser pointer.
It sold for $14.83, and the buyer knew it didn't work, proving early on that people will buy anything online.

Scooby-Doo was almost a sheepdog named Too Much.
The creators changed the character to a Great Dane and named him after the Frank Sinatra song, *Strangers in the Night*.

The original title of *Pulp Fiction* was *Black Mask*.
Quentin Tarantino considered naming the film after a popular crime magazine but ultimately opted for its now-iconic title.

Batman's Joker was inspired by a silent film.
The character's appearance and personality were heavily influenced by Conrad Veidt's performance in *The Man Who Laughs* (1928).

The voice of Bugs Bunny didn't like carrots.
Mel Blanc, who voiced the famous rabbit, would spit out bites of carrots after recording to avoid choking.

The first-ever sitcom was *Mary Kay and Johnny*.
This pioneering show aired in 1947 and focused on the everyday lives of a married couple.

The most expensive comic book sold for $3.6 million.
A near-mint copy of *Action Comics No. 1*, which introduced Superman, set the record in 2021.

Eminem holds the record for the fastest rap verse.
In *Godzilla*, Eminem raps 225 words in just 30 seconds, demonstrating his unmatched lyrical speed.

The theme song for *Jeopardy!* was written in under a minute.
Merv Griffin composed the iconic tune in 1963 as a lullaby for his son, and it's since become a trivia staple.

The *Game of Thrones* Iron Throne was made of real swords.
The iconic prop was crafted from hundreds of swords, though they were dulled for safety.

The first book ever sold on Amazon was about artificial intelligence.
Titled *Fluid Concepts and Creative Analogies*, it was purchased in 1995, starting Amazon's path to becoming a retail giant.

The phrase "Netflix and chill" started as a joke.
What began as a literal reference to watching Netflix became a popular euphemism for casual hangouts—or more.

Wolverine was almost a genetically mutated wolverine.
Early drafts of the character's backstory suggested he was an actual animal mutated into a human-like form.

The creator of Wonder Woman also invented the lie detector.
William Moulton Marston's interest in truth and justice extended beyond comics, as he helped develop the polygraph machine.

The original Barbie had a full name.
Barbara Millicent Roberts, named after the creator's daughter, debuted in 1959 as the ultimate fashion doll.

The most-watched Netflix show is *Squid Game*.
With over 1.6 billion hours viewed in its first 28 days, the Korean survival drama shattered streaming records.

The name "Pikachu" is based on Japanese onomatopoeia.
"Pika" refers to an electric spark, while "chu" mimics a mouse's squeak, perfectly describing the Pokémon mascot.

The first feature-length movie was Australian.
Released in 1906, *The Story of the Kelly Gang* was the world's first full-length narrative film.

The highest-paid actor of all time is Robert Downey Jr.
His earnings from the Marvel Cinematic Universe, particularly *Avengers: Endgame*, exceed $400 million.

The *Seinfeld* pilot was almost canceled.
Executives doubted the show's appeal, calling it "too New York." It later became one of the most successful sitcoms ever.

The word "Simpsons" appears in every episode's opening credits.
It's subtly written on the cash register when Maggie is scanned.

Shrek has a star on the Hollywood Walk of Fame.
The lovable ogre was honored in 2010 for his cultural impact, alongside iconic human celebrities.

E.T.'s face was modeled after Albert Einstein and a pug.
The combination of the famous physicist and the wrinkly dog created the alien's distinct look.

Will Smith turned down *The Matrix* to star in *Wild Wild West*.
Smith passed on the iconic sci-fi role of Neo, a decision he has openly joked about regretting.

The original *Star Wars* script was rejected 44 times.
George Lucas faced rejection after rejection before 20th Century Fox finally gave the galaxy far, far away a chance.

The Hulk was originally gray.
In the first comic, the Hulk was gray, but printing issues led to inconsistencies, so Marvel changed him to green.

The *Harry Potter* films used over 250,000 wands.
From duels to classes, the props department crafted and replaced an enormous number of wands during the series.

The longest movie ever made is 85 hours long.
Titled *Logistics*, this Swedish film explores the life cycle of a pedometer, from production to retail.

There's a secret McDonald's in *Thor: Ragnarok*.
The set for Sakaar includes a piece of McDonald's signage hidden in the junkyard, an Easter egg for sharp-eyed fans.

Darth Vader only appears for 12 minutes in *A New Hope*.
Despite being one of cinema's most iconic villains, Vader's screen time in the first *Star Wars* movie is shockingly brief.

The longest-running film in theaters is *The Rocky Horror Picture Show*.
The 1975 cult classic still plays in midnight showings around the world, making it a cinematic phenomenon.

The Millennium Falcon's design was inspired by a hamburger.
George Lucas based the iconic starship's round shape on a burger he saw while brainstorming concepts.

Elvis Presley only won three Grammys.
Despite his legendary career, The King's Grammy wins were all for gospel music, not rock and roll.

The Joker has won two Oscars.
Heath Ledger and Joaquin Phoenix both received Academy Awards for their portrayals of the iconic DC villain.

The Pixar lamp has a name.
The famous desk lamp is called Luxo Jr., named after Pixar's first short film from 1986.

Tom Hanks was the first actor considered for Jerry Maguire.
Before Tom Cruise landed the role, Cameron Crowe wrote the part with Hanks in mind, but Hanks was busy directing *That Thing You Do!*.

The *Friends* fountain is also in *Hocus Pocus*.
The fountain featured in the sitcom's opening credits appears in the Halloween classic as well, located on the Warner Bros. lot.

The most-viewed video on YouTube is "Baby Shark."
This catchy children's tune surpassed 12 billion views, making it the most-watched video in YouTube history.

The Office had a failed pilot in the UK before the US version.
The original *Office* creator, Ricky Gervais, scrapped the first attempt at an American adaptation, leading to the now-famous version.

Breaking Bad's Walter White is based on a real person.
While not a drug kingpin, a chemistry teacher named Walter White was arrested for making methamphetamine in Alabama in 2008.

Jack Nicholson was paid a percentage of Batman profits.
Nicholson's deal to play the Joker in the 1989 film earned him over $50 million, thanks to box office and merchandise sales.

Superman once fought Muhammad Ali.
The 1978 comic *Superman vs. Muhammad Ali* featured the Man of Steel boxing the real-life heavyweight champ.

The Oscars were almost called "The Golden Statuettes."
The nickname "Oscar" caught on after a librarian at the Academy said it looked like her uncle Oscar.

The Godfather horse head was real.
The famous scene where a severed horse head appears in a bed used an actual head from a slaughterhouse, shocking the actors and audience.

Stan Lee's favorite Marvel cameo was in Thor: Ragnarok.
Lee loved his role as the barber who cuts Thor's hair, calling it one of his funniest appearances.

Will Ferrell and John C. Reilly learned to play instruments for *Step Brothers*.
Both actors took lessons to perform their musical scenes, including the hilarious
Boats 'n Hoes number.

The *Game of Thrones* Iron Throne has swords from *The Lord of the Rings*.
Peter Jackson's production team donated swords from their movies to be included in
the throne's design.

Arnold Schwarzenegger was paid $21,428 per word for *Terminator 2*.
With just 700 words of dialogue and a $15 million paycheck, each word cost more
than most people's cars.

The *Avengers* cast got matching tattoos.
After filming *Infinity War*, five of the six original Avengers actors got tattoos to
commemorate their time in the MCU.

Stephen King's *It* was inspired by his childhood.
King's fear of clowns and memories of exploring drainage tunnels shaped the
terrifying novel.

The *Lord of the Rings* cast formed a lifelong bond.
Many of the actors, including Elijah Wood and Ian McKellen, still wear matching
tattoos of the Elvish number "9" for their fellowship.

The Hogwarts Express train is real.
The Jacobite steam train, featured in the *Harry Potter* films, operates in Scotland
and is a popular tourist attraction.

James Cameron sketched the Titanic sinking as a child.
Obsessed with shipwrecks, Cameron drew images of the Titanic long before directing the iconic film.

Leonardo DiCaprio improvised the glass scene in *Django Unchained*.
When he accidentally cut his hand, DiCaprio stayed in character, adding an intense realism to the scene.

The DeLorean from *Back to the Future* was almost a refrigerator.
The time machine was originally written as a refrigerator but was changed to a car for practical (and safety) reasons.

***Frozen's* "Let It Go" was written in one day.**
Kristen Anderson-Lopez and Robert Lopez composed the hit song in just one afternoon, not knowing it would become a global anthem.

The *Pulp Fiction* briefcase was never supposed to be mysterious.
Originally, the briefcase contained diamonds, but Quentin Tarantino left it ambiguous for fun, creating endless fan theories.

The name "Homer Simpson" came from the creator's father.
Matt Groening named Homer after his own dad, while other *Simpsons* family members were named after his relatives.

Mr. T started his career as a bodyguard.
Before becoming a pop culture icon, Mr. T protected celebrities like Muhammad Ali and Michael Jackson.

The first Pixar film was *Luxo Jr.*
The 1986 short about a hopping desk lamp was Pixar's debut, introducing its now-famous animation style.

The Matrix code is based on sushi recipes.
The iconic green code cascading down the screen was created by scanning characters from a sushi cookbook.

Marilyn Monroe owned over 400 books.
Despite her "dumb blonde" persona, Monroe was an avid reader with a library spanning philosophy, literature, and poetry.

The *Toy Story* script was rewritten mid-production.
Early drafts made Woody unlikeable, so the character was reimagined as the lovable leader we know today.

The *Stranger Things* Demogorgon was inspired by *Dungeons & Dragons*.
The show's monster shares its name with a creature from the classic tabletop game, tying the series to its 80s roots.

The Lion King was almost called King of the Jungle.
The name changed when animators realized lions don't actually live in jungles, making the title inaccurate.

Freddie Mercury designed Queen's logo.
The band's iconic crest, featuring zodiac symbols for its members, was created by Mercury, who studied graphic design.

The *Avengers: Endgame* script was kept so secret, even the actors didn't know the ending.

Tom Holland, known for spoiling surprises, was given fake scenes to avoid leaks.

Winnie the Pooh is based on a real bear.

A bear named Winnipeg inspired the beloved character, and Christopher Robin's stuffed animals brought the rest of the gang to life.

Alfred Hitchcock never won an Oscar.

Despite being one of the greatest directors in history, Hitchcock never took home a competitive Academy Award.

SPORTS AND GAMES

Unbelievable records and bizarre moments in sports and gaming.

Basketball was invented with a soccer ball and peach baskets.
Dr. James Naismith created the game in 1891, using peach baskets as goals because there were no proper hoops yet.

The Olympic Games used to give medals for art.
From 1912 to 1948, the Olympics awarded medals in categories like literature, painting, and architecture alongside athletic events.

The longest tennis match lasted 11 hours and 5 minutes.
In the 2010 Wimbledon tournament, John Isner defeated Nicolas Mahut in a marathon match that spanned three days.

Golf is the only sport played on the Moon.
In 1971, astronaut Alan Shepard hit two golf balls on the lunar surface during the Apollo 14 mission.

The Stanley Cup has a typo.
It reads "Toronto Maple Leafs" as "Toronto Maple Leaes," proving even the most prestigious trophies aren't immune to human error.

A single baseball game can use up to 120 balls.
Between foul balls, home runs, and scuffed pitches, a Major League Baseball game goes through dozens of balls every nine innings.

The first modern Olympic Games featured no gold medals.
Athletes in the 1896 Athens Olympics received silver medals for first place and copper for second.

Table tennis balls can curve like a soccer ball.
A phenomenon called the Magnus effect allows skilled players to create incredible spins and curves in table tennis matches.

A chess match once lasted 20 hours.
The longest official chess game on record was played in 1989 and ended in a draw after 269 moves.

Marathon distances weren't always 26.2 miles.
The original marathon was approximately 25 miles, but the 1908 London Olympics extended it to 26.2 to finish in front of the royal box.

The fastest red card in soccer history was after 2 seconds.
In 2000, Lee Todd was sent off for swearing immediately after the referee's whistle started the game.

The NFL uses 700,000 footballs each season.
That's enough leather to make a football field's worth of footballs—literally.

Polo is the oldest team sport.
Dating back to 600 BC in Persia, polo holds the record as the oldest known team-based competition.

Cricket games can last up to 5 days.
Test matches, the longest format of cricket, often end in a draw after days of intense play.

The World Cup is the most-watched sporting event.
The FIFA World Cup draws an audience of over 3.5 billion people—almost half the planet's population.

The first Super Bowl tickets cost $6.
In 1967, the inaugural Super Bowl between the Packers and Chiefs offered affordable tickets compared to today's thousands.

A perfect bowling score is incredibly rare.
The odds of a casual bowler rolling a perfect 300 game are roughly 1 in 11,500.

Professional chess players can burn 6,000 calories a day.
Intense mental effort during tournaments can raise heart rates and stress levels, leading to significant calorie burn.

The Tour de France is over 2,000 miles long.
Cyclists in this legendary race cover incredible distances through grueling mountain stages and scenic countryside.

Baseball umpires used to sit in rocking chairs.
In the 19th century, umpires were stationed far from home plate and watched the game from chairs.

The inventor of volleyball also invented a fire escape.
William G. Morgan, who created volleyball in 1895, also held patents for safety and fire equipment.

Ping pong is an Olympic sport.
Introduced in 1988, table tennis has become a highly competitive Olympic event featuring amazing skill and reflexes.

The longest recorded soccer match lasted 108 hours.
Played in the UK in 2016, this marathon charity game set a record for the longest soccer match in history.

The NBA used to play with cages around the court.
In basketball's early days, wire mesh cages surrounded courts to prevent fans from interfering with the game.

The fastest pitch in MLB history was 105.1 mph.
Aroldis Chapman threw this blazing fastball in 2010, earning him the nickname "The Cuban Missile."

Hockey pucks are frozen before games.
Chilling the pucks prevents them from bouncing and ensures a smoother glide on the ice.

The Olympic torch has been carried underwater.
During the 2000 Sydney Games, the flame was transported through the Great Barrier Reef by a scuba diver.

Michael Phelps has more Olympic golds than 161 countries.
With 23 gold medals, Phelps outranks the gold medal counts of many entire nations in Olympic history.

Basketball rims have been 10 feet high since 1891.
The height hasn't changed since the game's invention, even as players have grown taller and more athletic.

Tug of war used to be an Olympic event.
From 1900 to 1920, this team strength competition was a legitimate Olympic sport.

The longest golf hole in the world is 1,097 yards.
Located in South Korea, the par-7 3rd hole at Gunsan Country Club challenges even the best golfers.

A soccer ball has 32 panels.
The standard design, consisting of 20 hexagons and 12 pentagons, was introduced for better aerodynamics.

Billiards was banned in England in the 15th century.
King Henry VII outlawed the game, believing it distracted soldiers from their duties.

Table tennis balls used to be made of cork.
In the sport's early days, players used cork balls before switching to celluloid for better bounce.

The first recorded Olympics had only one event.
The ancient games in 776 BC featured a single footrace known as the *stadion*, roughly 192 meters long.

The Chicago Cubs' goat curse lasted 71 years.
Legend has it that a billy goat curse prevented the Cubs from winning the World Series from 1945 to 2016.

The longest recorded volleyball rally lasted 132 touches.
This record-breaking rally occurred during a professional game in South Korea in 2013.

Soccer balls were once made from pig bladders.
Before modern materials, early soccer balls were crafted using inflated animal bladders, making them less durable.

The first FIFA World Cup trophy disappeared.
The Jules Rimet Trophy was stolen in 1966 but later found by a dog named Pickles in a bush.

Table tennis was invented as a parlor game.
The sport began as an after-dinner pastime in Victorian England, played with books as paddles and a ball made of string.

The first hockey pucks were made of frozen cow dung.
Early players improvised with what they had, including frozen manure, before standardized rubber pucks were introduced.

The Olympic rings symbolize global unity.
The five rings represent the five inhabited continents, with their colors found in every national flag.

Shaquille O'Neal has broken over 20 basketball backboards.
His powerful dunks led to reinforced backboards being mandated in the NBA.

Chess is over 1,500 years old.
The game originated in India around the 6th century and has evolved into one of the world's most enduring competitions.

The fastest tennis serve on record was 163.7 mph.
Australian player Sam Groth achieved this blistering serve in 2012, setting an unbeatable standard.

The first Olympic marathon winner ran barefoot.
In 1896, Spyridon Louis, a Greek water carrier, won the first modern marathon without wearing shoes.

The Green Bay Packers are the only publicly owned NFL team.
Unlike other franchises, the Packers are owned by their fans through shares sold by the team.

The Olympic gold medal isn't pure gold.
Since 1912, gold medals have been mostly silver, with only a thin layer of gold plating.

Chess was once a sport in the Olympics.
Though it hasn't been included in recent games, chess was an official part of the 1924 Summer Olympics.

The longest basketball shot was made from 114 feet.
Thunder Law of the Harlem Globetrotters set this record in 2016, sinking an unbelievable full-court shot.

The first video game tournament was in 1972.
Stanford University hosted a competition for the game *Spacewar!*, offering a subscription to *Rolling Stone* magazine as the prize.

The fastest 100-meter sprint was completed in 9.58 seconds.
Usain Bolt set this world record at the 2009 World Athletics Championships in Berlin.

Soccer is the most popular sport in the world.
With over 4 billion fans, soccer is the undisputed global favorite, played and watched on every continent.

The first recorded baseball game was in 1846.
It took place in Hoboken, New Jersey, between the Knickerbocker Club and the New York Nine.

The first video game console was called the Magnavox Odyssey.
Released in 1972, it predates Atari's Pong and started the home gaming revolution.

Michael Jordan once retired to play baseball.
After his first retirement from basketball, Jordan joined the minor leagues, playing for the Birmingham Barons.

Serena Williams holds the most Grand Slam titles in the Open Era.
Her 23 major singles titles make her one of the greatest athletes of all time.

Football helmets were originally made of leather.
Introduced in the early 1900s, leather helmets offered minimal protection compared to today's high-tech designs.

The longest cricket match lasted 10 days.
In 1939, England and South Africa played a Test match so long it had to end as a draw when the English team needed to catch their boat home.

Video games generate more revenue than movies and music combined.
The gaming industry earns over $180 billion annually, dwarfing other entertainment sectors.

Ping pong paddles are covered with rubber for spin.
The addition of rubber allowed players to add spin and control, revolutionizing the sport in the 1950s.

Chess grandmasters can think 10 moves ahead.
Top players visualize intricate game scenarios far in advance, often memorizing thousands of potential strategies.

A perfect game in baseball is one of the rarest achievements.
It's happened only 23 times in Major League Baseball history, requiring flawless pitching and defense.

Formula 1 drivers experience up to 5G forces.
In high-speed turns, drivers endure extreme gravitational forces, similar to fighter jet pilots.

The first Wimbledon championship took place in 1877.
The oldest tennis tournament in the world began as a local gentlemen's event with only 22 players.

Shaquille O'Neal only made one three-point shot in his NBA career.
Despite his dominance in the paint, Shaq's long-range shooting was almost non-existent.

The heaviest sumo wrestler weighed over 600 pounds.
Konishiki Yasokichi, nicknamed "The Dump Truck," was a dominant force in the ring and one of the sport's heaviest athletes.

The first televised sports event was a baseball game.
In 1939, NBC broadcast a college baseball game between Columbia and Princeton, marking the beginning of sports on TV.

Babe Ruth once pitched a 14-inning complete game.
Before becoming a legendary slugger, Ruth was an incredible pitcher, throwing this marathon game in 1916.

The Stanley Cup has been to the bottom of a swimming pool.
Hockey players have celebrated with the Cup in all sorts of ways, including using it as a pool toy.

The fastest goal in soccer history was scored in 2.4 seconds.
Nawaf Al-Abed achieved this lightning-fast goal during a Saudi league match in 2009.

The most holes-in-one in a single round is five.
Norman Manley set this improbable golf record in 1964, defying astronomical odds.

A chessboard has more possible moves than atoms in the universe.
The game's complexity creates an almost infinite number of potential positions, making it a lifelong challenge.

Table tennis is the fastest ball sport.
With ball speeds reaching 70 mph in a small area, it's one of the most fast-paced and reaction-intensive games.

The Super Bowl is the most-watched annual event in the U.S.
Over 100 million Americans tune in each year, with the halftime show often rivaling the game in popularity.

Muhammad Ali's gloves from the "Fight of the Century" sold for $836,500.
The iconic gloves he wore against Joe Frazier became one of the most valuable pieces of sports memorabilia.

The FIFA World Cup trophy is 18-karat gold.
Weighing over 13 pounds, it's one of the most prestigious and expensive trophies in sports.

The Olympic flame is never extinguished.
The flame is reignited before each Olympics using a backup flame lit from the previous Games, symbolizing continuity.

Chess was banned in Iran for 20 years.
Following the Iranian Revolution, chess was prohibited until 1988, when it was declared compatible with Islamic principles.

Baseball was originally called "rounders."
The sport evolved from a 19th-century British game before becoming America's pastime.

The longest home run ever hit traveled 582 feet.
Joey Meyer of the Denver Zephyrs smashed this record-breaking homer in 1987.

The oldest Olympic athlete was 72 years old.
Swedish shooter Oscar Swahn competed in the 1920 Games, proving age is just a number.

Basketball was introduced to the Olympics by a women's team.
The sport debuted in the 1904 St. Louis Games, with female players demonstrating the new game.

The chess clock was invented in 1883.
Before that, matches could drag on indefinitely without time restrictions, frustrating players and spectators.

The most expensive video game ever developed was *Grand Theft Auto V*.
With a $265 million budget, it became one of the most successful entertainment products of all time.

The Chicago Bulls won every NBA Finals they played in.
During Michael Jordan's tenure, the Bulls went 6-for-6 in the Finals, a perfect record.

The FIFA World Cup has been held every four years since 1930.
The tournament has only been canceled twice, during World War II in 1942 and 1946.

The term "hat trick" originated in cricket.
It referred to a bowler taking three wickets in three consecutive deliveries, often rewarded with a hat from their team.

Bowling dates back over 5,000 years.
Archaeologists discovered a form of bowling in an Egyptian tomb, making it one of the world's oldest sports.

The Harlem Globetrotters were originally a serious team.
Before becoming entertainers, they were a competitive basketball team that won over 100 straight games in the 1940s.

The heaviest wrestling title belt weighed over 20 pounds.
The Big Gold Belt, used in WCW and WWE, is one of the largest and heaviest championship belts ever made.

The first World Series was played in 1903.
The Boston Americans (now Red Sox) defeated the Pittsburgh Pirates in a best-of-nine series to claim the championship.

The FIFA World Cup trophy was stolen in 1966.
It was recovered a week later by a dog named Pickles, who found it wrapped in newspaper in a garden.

The Olympic flag debuted in 1920.
The iconic five rings made their first appearance in Antwerp, symbolizing the unity of the five inhabited continents.

Baseball umpires didn't always wear protective gear.
Before 1970, many umpires called games without facemasks or chest protectors, risking serious injuries.

The first televised NBA game was in 1953.
The game featured the Boston Celtics and the Fort Wayne Pistons, bringing professional basketball to a national audience.

The highest-scoring NBA game ended 186–184.
The Denver Nuggets and Detroit Pistons set the record for the most points in a game in 1983, including three overtimes.

The first official cricket match was in 1844.
Played between the USA and Canada, it remains one of the oldest international sporting events.

The longest-running college football rivalry is between Lehigh and Lafayette.
Dating back to 1884, this rivalry has been played more than 150 times, making it a cornerstone of college sports history.

The fastest hockey slapshot was 118.3 mph.
Zdeno Chara, the towering defenseman, set this record during the 2012 NHL All-Star Skills Competition.

The first Super Bowl halftime show featured college marching bands.
Before the era of superstar performances, the 1967 halftime show showcased the University of Arizona and Grambling State bands.

The first Olympic mascot was a dachshund.
Waldi, the colorful dog, was introduced during the 1972 Munich Olympics, marking the beginning of mascots in the Games.

Table tennis players can hit the ball at over 60 mph.
The combination of speed and spin makes professional table tennis a high-stakes and lightning-fast sport.

The longest football game lasted 82 minutes in overtime.
In 1971, the Dolphins and Chiefs played an epic playoff game that ended with a Miami victory.

Chessboxing combines brains and brawn.
This hybrid sport alternates between rounds of chess and boxing, challenging both the mind and body.

The shortest boxing match lasted four seconds.
In 1946, Mike Collins knocked out Pat Brownson with the first punch of the fight, setting an unbeatable record.

The oldest horse racing event is the Palio di Siena.
Dating back to 1633 in Italy, this bareback horse race is still a popular tradition.

Basketball was originally played with nine players per team.
Dr. James Naismith's original rules allowed for nine players on the court instead of today's five.

The first professional baseball team was the Cincinnati Red Stockings.
Founded in 1869, they were the first team to pay all players a salary.

The first Olympic Games with female athletes was in 1900.
Women participated in sports like tennis and sailing, breaking barriers for future generations.

The longest continuous golf hole is 1,082 yards.
This par-7 monster is located at Satsuki Golf Club in Japan, challenging even the longest hitters.

The Stanley Cup has been to space.
In 1999, astronaut John Glenn took a replica of the Cup aboard the Space Shuttle Discovery.

Bowling was an exhibition sport in the 1988 Olympics.
Though it didn't make the official lineup, bowling had its moment in the spotlight during the Seoul Games.

The term "love" in tennis means zero.
The origin is unclear, but one theory suggests it comes from the French word *l'oeuf*, meaning "egg," resembling a zero.

The first video game, *Tennis for Two*, was created in 1958.
Developed by physicist William Higinbotham, this simple game was played on an oscilloscope.

The longest home run streak lasted eight games.
Dale Long of the Pittsburgh Pirates set the record in 1956, later tied by Don Mattingly and Ken Griffey Jr.

A soccer referee once showed a red card to himself.
In 1998, English referee Melvin Sylvester accidentally sent himself off after losing his temper during a match.

The fastest hat trick in hockey was scored in 21 seconds.
Bill Mosienko of the Chicago Blackhawks achieved this incredible feat in 1952.

Basketball's three-point line wasn't introduced until 1979.
The addition of the arc revolutionized the game, creating new strategies and specialists.

The most expensive chess set costs $1.65 million.
Designed by Charles Hollander, this luxurious set features gold and diamonds, making it a true collector's item.

A cricket ball is harder than a baseball.
Weighing about 5.75 ounces, a cricket ball can cause serious injuries if not handled properly.

TECHNOLOGY THROUGH TIME

Surprising origins and uses of technology.

The first programmable computer was built in 1936.
Konrad Zuse's Z3, created in Nazi Germany, was the world's first programmable digital computer and laid the foundation for modern computing.

The internet was almost called the "Information Superhighway."
Before settling on "internet," early developers debated using this now-retro term to describe the global network.

The first email was sent in 1971.
Computer engineer Ray Tomlinson sent the first email to himself, experimenting with the new "@" symbol.

The telephone was originally called the "harmonic telegraph."
Alexander Graham Bell's groundbreaking invention in 1876 was initially thought of as a musical communication device.

The first photograph took 8 hours to expose.
In 1826, Joseph Nicéphore Niépce captured the first permanent photograph, but you had to be patient—it took all day.

The first text message said "Merry Christmas."
Sent in 1992 by engineer Neil Papworth, this simple holiday greeting marked the beginning of SMS communication.

The original Apple computer was built in a garage.
Steve Jobs and Steve Wozniak famously assembled the Apple I in Jobs's parents' garage in 1976.

The Wright brothers' first flight lasted 12 seconds.
In 1903, Orville Wright piloted the world's first powered flight, covering 120 feet in less than half a minute.

The first television broadcast happened in 1928.
This historic broadcast by Charles Francis Jenkins featured a mechanical TV transmitting a moving image of a windmill.

GPS is free because of Ronald Reagan.
After a Korean airliner was shot down in 1983, Reagan ordered GPS technology be made freely available to civilians.

The first computer virus was a prank.
In 1986, two Pakistani brothers created the "Brain" virus to discourage software piracy. It displayed their contact info on infected screens.

The first video game was created in 1958.
Physicist William Higinbotham developed *Tennis for Two*, a simple game displayed on an oscilloscope.

The first website is still live.
Tim Berners-Lee's 1991 creation, *info.cern.ch*, introduced the world to the World Wide Web and is preserved as a historical artifact.

The first smartphone debuted in 1992.
IBM's "Simon" combined a touchscreen, calendar, and email capabilities—decades before the iPhone.

The first electric car was built in 1884.
Thomas Parker designed an early electric vehicle, proving that clean energy transportation isn't a new idea.

The world's first robot was built in the 15th century.
Leonardo da Vinci sketched a mechanical knight capable of sitting, waving, and moving its head.

The floppy disk was invented by IBM in 1967.
These early storage devices could hold a whopping 80 kilobytes—less than a single modern photo.

The first commercial computer weighed 29,000 pounds.
The UNIVAC I, introduced in 1951, required an entire room and cost over $1 million.

The first fax machine was patented in 1843.
Alexander Bain's "Electric Printing Telegraph" was a precursor to the office fax machines of the 20th century.

The first photograph of Earth from space was taken in 1946.
A camera aboard a V-2 rocket captured this groundbreaking image, changing humanity's perspective forever.

The world's first video call happened in 1964.
Bell Labs showcased video calling at the New York World's Fair, though it took decades to become mainstream.

The first electronic computer filled an entire room.
ENIAC, built in 1945, weighed 30 tons and used thousands of vacuum tubes for processing power.

The first 3D printer was created in 1984.
Chuck Hull invented stereolithography, the technology that would revolutionize manufacturing and medicine.

The first automatic dishwasher was invented in 1886.
Josephine Cochrane created a hand-powered device that used water pressure to clean dishes more efficiently.

Wi-Fi was invented by accident.
In 1992, Australian scientists developing radio signals for astronomy realized they had stumbled upon wireless internet technology.

The first typewriter keyboard was arranged alphabetically.
Christopher Sholes, its inventor, changed the layout to QWERTY in 1873 to prevent typebars from jamming.

The first ATM was introduced in 1967.
This revolutionary machine in London allowed customers to withdraw cash using a special coded voucher.

The first electric light predates Edison.
Humphry Davy demonstrated the first electric arc lamp in 1806, decades before Edison's famous bulb.

The microwave oven was discovered by accident.
Percy Spencer noticed a candy bar melting in his pocket while working on radar technology, leading to the invention of the microwave.

The first email spam was sent in 1978.
A marketer sent a mass message to 400 people advertising computer products, creating a digital annoyance that persists today.

The first barcode was inspired by Morse code.
Invented in 1951, the barcode uses extended and shortened lines to encode information like Morse dots and dashes.

The first electric battery was invented in 1800.
Alessandro Volta's voltaic pile consisted of zinc and copper discs separated by brine-soaked cloth.

The first movie ever shown was in 1895.
The Lumière brothers projected *Workers Leaving the Lumière Factory*, captivating audiences and marking the birth of cinema.

The first mechanical clock appeared in the 14th century.
These early clocks revolutionized timekeeping with gears, weights, and pendulums, replacing sundials and water clocks.

The first video uploaded to YouTube is still online.
Titled *Me at the zoo*, the 19-second video by co-founder Jawed Karim features him talking about elephants at the San Diego Zoo.

The first electronic calculator was the size of a desk.
Invented in 1961, it performed basic arithmetic and cost as much as a car.

The first electric guitar was nicknamed "The Frying Pan."
Invented by George Beauchamp in 1931, it had a round body that resembled a frying pan, sparking the electric music revolution.

The first text-to-speech software was created in the 1950s.
Bell Labs' "Audrey" could recognize spoken digits, laying the groundwork for modern voice assistants.

The first computer mouse was made of wood.
In 1964, Doug Engelbart designed the first mouse with a wooden shell and two metal wheels.

The first synthetic plastic was invented in 1907.
Bakelite, created by Leo Baekeland, launched the modern plastics industry with its heat-resistant properties.

The first artificial satellite was launched in 1957.
Sputnik 1, sent into orbit by the Soviet Union, was a metal sphere the size of a beach ball that changed the course of history.

The first radio broadcast was in 1906.
Reginald Fessenden transmitted a Christmas Eve program featuring music and a Bible reading, reaching ships at sea.

The first programmable thermostat was invented in 1906.
The "Honeywell Heating Specialty" allowed users to set their heating systems to operate on a timer, a precursor to today's smart thermostats.

The first electric elevator was built in 1880.
Werner von Siemens created the first powered elevator, a major step toward modern skyscrapers.

The first smartphone app store was launched in 2008.
Apple's App Store debuted with 500 apps, revolutionizing how we interact with mobile devices.

The first laser was described as "a solution in search of a problem."
When Theodore Maiman built the first laser in 1960, its practical uses were unclear—now it's in everything from printers to surgery.

The first "computer bug" was an actual moth.
In 1947, Grace Hopper discovered a moth stuck in the Harvard Mark II computer, coining the term "debugging."

The first phone call was between Alexander Graham Bell and his assistant.
On March 10, 1876, Bell called Watson with the words, "Mr. Watson, come here—I want to see you."

The first commercially available video game console cost $100.
Released in 1972, the Magnavox Odyssey was a luxury item, equivalent to over $650 today.

The Eiffel Tower was the tallest man-made structure until 1930.
It lost the title to the Chrysler Building in New York City, but not without inspiring countless innovations.

The first airplane meal was served in 1919.
Passengers flying from London to Paris received sandwiches, fruit, and coffee—a far cry from modern airline dining.

Bluetooth is named after a Viking king.
King Harald "Bluetooth" Gormsson united Denmark and Norway, inspiring the technology's name for uniting devices.

The first electric traffic light was installed in 1914.
Cleveland, Ohio, was the first city to use electric traffic signals to manage increasing automobile traffic.

The Apollo guidance computer had less power than a modern smartphone.
The technology that took astronauts to the Moon had just 4KB of memory—your phone likely has millions of times more.

The first artificial heart was implanted in 1982.
The Jarvik-7 kept patient Barney Clark alive for 112 days, marking a milestone in medical engineering.

The typewriter revolutionized office work in the 1860s.
Sholes & Glidden introduced the first commercially successful typewriter, transforming how documents were produced.

The first known mechanical calculator was invented in 1642.
Blaise Pascal designed the Pascaline, capable of performing basic addition and subtraction.

The first online purchase was a pizza.
In 1994, a customer ordered a pepperoni pizza with mushrooms and extra cheese using the internet—a precursor to modern e-commerce.

The floppy disk led to the USB drive.
Invented by IBM in 1967, floppy disks paved the way for compact, portable data storage.

The first text message emoji was sent in 1982.
Carnegie Mellon computer scientist Scott Fahlman used :-) to indicate humor, kickstarting emoji culture.

The first electric subway opened in 1890.
The London Underground's City & South London Railway became the first to use electric trains instead of steam-powered ones.

The first automobile was powered by steam.
In 1769, Nicolas-Joseph Cugnot built a steam-powered vehicle, which could travel at 2.5 mph.

The microwave oven was originally for radar research.
Percy Spencer's radar experiments led to the accidental discovery that microwaves could heat food.

The first ATM pin code was supposed to be six digits.
It was reduced to four digits because the inventor's wife, Caroline, could only remember four.

The first search engine was called Archie.
Developed in 1990, Archie indexed FTP files, laying the groundwork for modern search engines like Google.

The first transatlantic cable was laid in 1858.
This groundbreaking project enabled near-instant communication between North America and Europe.

The first mechanical pencil dates back to 1822.
Invented by Sampson Mordan, it introduced replaceable lead to writing instruments.

The first email spam law was enacted in 2003.
The U.S. CAN-SPAM Act aimed to reduce unsolicited emails but hasn't eradicated spam entirely.

The first airplane autopilot was invented in 1912.
Elmer Sperry created a gyroscopic device that allowed pilots to maintain a steady course.

The first wristwatch was made in 1868.
Patek Philippe crafted the watch for Countess Koscowicz, starting a trend that would dominate timekeeping.

The first voice recognition system was developed in 1952.
Bell Labs' "Audrey" could recognize spoken digits, a precursor to modern voice assistants like Siri and Alexa.

The first laser printer was invented in 1969.
Gary Starkweather at Xerox developed this revolutionary printer, now a standard in offices worldwide.

The first electric vacuum cleaner was invented in 1908.
James Spangler's "suction sweeper" became the prototype for modern vacuum cleaners.

The first television remote control was called "Lazy Bones."
Introduced in 1950 by Zenith, it was connected to the TV by a long cord.

The first film with CGI was *Westworld* (1973).
The sci-fi classic used computer-generated imagery to depict a robot's point of view.

The first solar-powered calculator debuted in 1978.
The Sharp EL-8026 introduced solar power to consumer electronics, sparking eco-friendly innovation.

The first video camera weighed over 1,000 pounds.
Invented in the 1920s, the RCA Photophone captured moving pictures but required a team to operate.

The first electric washing machine was patented in 1908.
Alva J. Fisher's invention made household chores significantly easier for millions of families.

The first airplane with a pressurized cabin flew in 1938.
The Boeing 307 Stratoliner allowed passengers to fly above turbulence for a smoother ride.

The first digital camera was built in 1975.
Steven Sasson's Kodak prototype captured black-and-white images at 0.01 megapixels.

The first fiber optic cable was installed in 1977.
This groundbreaking technology made high-speed, long-distance data transmission possible.

The first artificial satellite had no propulsion.
Sputnik 1 relied on Earth's gravity to orbit and transmitted simple radio pulses.

The first calculator watch debuted in the 1970s.
Casio's C-80 combined a digital watch with a mini calculator, embodying tech innovation of the era.

The first smartphone camera was introduced in 2000.
Sharp's J-SH04 featured a 0.11-megapixel camera, marking the start of the smartphone photography revolution.

The first 3D movie required special glasses.
1922's *The Power of Love* was the first 3D film, using polarized lenses to create the illusion of depth.

The first electric toaster was invented in 1893.
Crompton & Company created the first device to evenly toast bread slices.

The first GPS satellite launched in 1978.
Part of the NAVSTAR system, this satellite laid the foundation for modern navigation.

The first artificial intelligence program was written in 1956.
The "Logic Theorist" could solve mathematical problems, marking the birth of AI.

The first computer game was a tic-tac-toe simulator.
Developed in 1952, *OXO* ran on the EDSAC computer and was one of the earliest examples of gaming.

The first electric fan was invented in 1882.
Schuyler Wheeler's design brought relief to hot summer days and revolutionized indoor cooling.

The first email was sent to just one person.
Ray Tomlinson sent the first-ever email to himself as a test of the new messaging system.

The first automobile race took place in 1895.
The race, held in France, covered 732 miles and attracted enormous crowds.

The first color photograph was taken in 1861.
Physicist James Clerk Maxwell used a three-color process to create the world's first color image of a tartan ribbon.

The first ATM required customers to carry tokens.
When ATMs debuted in the 1960s, users inserted a special token to access their accounts.

The first sound recording was made in 1857.
Édouard-Léon Scott de Martinville recorded sound waves on a phonautograph but lacked the technology to play them back.

The first recorded use of the wheel was in 3500 BC.
The wheel, invented in Mesopotamia, initially served as a potter's tool before transforming transportation.

The first personal computer was the Altair 8800.
Released in 1975, this kit-based PC inspired Bill Gates and Paul Allen to create Microsoft.

The first commercially successful steam engine was invented in 1712.
Thomas Newcomen's engine revolutionized mining and laid the groundwork for the Industrial Revolution.

The first fax machine was created in 1843.
Alexander Bain's invention transmitted images over telegraph lines, marking the beginning of fax technology.

The first electric guitar solo was played in 1932.
Guitarist Eddie Durham showcased the revolutionary instrument, forever changing the music industry.

The first automatic sewing machine was invented in 1846.
Elias Howe patented the device, which dramatically increased productivity in garment making.

The first home video game console with interchangeable cartridges was the Fairchild Channel F.
Released in 1976, it allowed players to swap games—a feature we take for granted today.

The first successful parachute jump was in 1797.
André-Jacques Garnerin leapt from a hot-air balloon, safely landing and proving the concept.

The first electric motor was built in 1821.
Michael Faraday's invention demonstrated the principles of electromagnetism and inspired countless innovations.

The first radar system was invented in 1935.
Robert Watson-Watt's creation helped Britain detect enemy aircraft during World War II.

The first vacuum tube was invented in 1904.
John Ambrose Fleming's diode revolutionized electronics, leading to the development of radios and early computers.

The first vinyl record was pressed in 1948.
Columbia Records introduced the 12-inch LP, forever changing how we listen to music.

The first mobile phone call was made in 1973.
Martin Cooper of Motorola called a rival company to boast about his invention during a stroll in New York City.

The first electric power plant opened in 1882.
Thomas Edison's Pearl Street Station in New York City provided electricity to 59 customers.

The first wind turbine for electricity was built in 1887.
Scottish engineer James Blyth powered his home with a wind-powered generator, the precursor to today's wind farms.

The first commercially available typewriter was the Sholes and Glidden.
Released in 1874, it introduced the QWERTY keyboard layout still used today.

FOOD AND DRINK MYSTERIES

Unusual histories and surprising trivia about what we eat and drink.

Honey never spoils.
Archaeologists have found 3,000-year-old pots of honey in ancient Egyptian tombs that are still perfectly edible. Thanks to its low moisture content and acidity, honey is nature's eternal sweetener.

Ketchup was once sold as medicine.
In the 1830s, Dr. John Cook Bennett marketed ketchup as a cure for indigestion, creating pills made from concentrated tomato paste.

Pineapples take two years to grow.
Each pineapple plant produces only one fruit at a time, and the process from planting to harvest can take up to 24 months.

Lobsters were once considered poor man's food.
In colonial America, lobsters were so plentiful that they were fed to prisoners and servants, earning the nickname "poor man's protein."

Bananas are technically berries.
Botanically speaking, bananas meet the criteria for berries, while strawberries, surprisingly, do not.

Potatoes were the first vegetable grown in space.
In 1995, NASA experimented with growing potatoes aboard the Space Shuttle Columbia to explore sustainable space farming.

Peanuts aren't nuts.
They're legumes, more closely related to beans and lentils than walnuts or almonds.

Chocolate was once used as currency.
The ancient Mayans and Aztecs valued cacao beans so highly that they used them to trade for goods and services.

The most expensive coffee is made from cat poop.
Kopi luwak, made from beans digested and excreted by civet cats, can cost up to $600 per pound.

Cheese is older than recorded history.
Evidence of cheese-making dates back over 7,000 years, making it one of humanity's oldest food inventions.

Carrots were originally purple.
Before the 17th century, most carrots were purple, red, or yellow. The orange variety we know today was selectively bred in the Netherlands.

The world's hottest pepper can kill you.
The Carolina Reaper is so spicy that consuming too much at once could trigger anaphylactic shock.

Coca-Cola used to contain cocaine.
Until 1904, the original recipe for Coca-Cola included coca leaf extract, which naturally contains the drug.

Popcorn is over 5,000 years old.
Ancient popcorn remnants have been discovered in Peruvian caves, proving humans have been snacking on it for millennia.

Honey is made from nectar and bee vomit.
Bees digest nectar in their stomachs, regurgitate it, and pass it between each other until it becomes honey.

Pufferfish can kill you if prepared incorrectly.
Known as fugu in Japan, this delicacy must be carefully prepared to remove its deadly toxin, which is 1,200 times more lethal than cyanide.

There's a fruit that tastes like chocolate pudding.
The black sapote, also known as the "chocolate pudding fruit," has a flavor and texture remarkably similar to chocolate custard.

A single strand of spaghetti is called a spaghetto.
The word "spaghetti" is plural in Italian, with "spaghetto" referring to just one noodle.

Watermelon is 92% water.
This refreshing fruit lives up to its name, making it a natural hydration source in hot weather.

Peppers don't actually burn your mouth.
The heat from chili peppers comes from capsaicin, which tricks your brain into thinking your mouth is on fire.

Vanilla comes from orchids.
Vanilla beans are the fruit of a specific type of orchid, and harvesting them is so labor-intensive that they're the second most expensive spice after saffron.

Apples are part of the rose family.
Along with pears, cherries, and peaches, apples are members of the Rosaceae family, sharing a botanical lineage with roses.

The hole in a pasta spoon measures a single serving.
That round hole in the center of a spaghetti spoon is designed to measure out one portion of uncooked pasta.

The world's largest omelet required 145,000 eggs.
This massive culinary feat was achieved in Portugal in 2012, weighing in at over 6 tons.

Mushrooms are more closely related to humans than plants.
Genetically speaking, fungi share more DNA with animals than they do with plants, making them a unique kingdom of life.

Bubblegum is pink because it was the only color available.
The original bubblegum, created in 1928, was dyed pink simply because it was the only food coloring on hand.

There's a sparkling tea made from ants.
In Denmark, a Michelin-starred restaurant uses ants to create a fizzy tea with a citrusy flavor, showcasing nature's creativity.

The red food dye carmine is made from bugs.
This common dye, found in candies and drinks, is made by crushing cochineal insects.

Rice can be used to clean coffee grinders.
Running uncooked rice through a grinder removes oils and residue, leaving it clean and ready for your next brew.

Maple syrup was discovered by accident.
According to legend, Native Americans noticed sap dripping from a maple tree and boiling into a sweet syrup.

Arachibutyrophobia is the fear of peanut butter sticking to the roof of your mouth.
While it sounds funny, this phobia is very real for some people.

The world's largest pizza was over 13,000 square feet.
Made in Rome in 2012, the pizza was gluten-free and required 48 hours to complete.

The oldest wine in the world is over 1,650 years old.
The Speyer wine bottle, discovered in Germany, dates back to around 325 AD and remains unopened.

Nutmeg can be hallucinogenic.
In large amounts, this common spice can induce psychoactive effects due to a compound called myristicin.

Avocados are berries.
Botanically, avocados are classified as berries because they have a single seed enclosed by fleshy fruit.

Pineapples were once a status symbol.
In 18th-century Europe, pineapples were so rare and expensive that they were rented as table decorations.

Sugar was once considered a spice.
Before becoming a common sweetener, sugar was classified alongside rare and valuable spices like cinnamon and nutmeg.

A raw oyster is still alive when you eat it.
Fresh oysters are kept alive until consumption to ensure they're safe to eat and at their peak flavor.

Spam is Hawaii's favorite meat.
Hawaiians consume more Spam per capita than any other state, thanks to its introduction during World War II.

Coffee was once banned in several countries.
In the 16th and 17th centuries, coffee was outlawed in regions like Mecca and Italy due to its stimulating effects.

The world's most expensive spice is saffron.
Harvested from the crocus flower, saffron's labor-intensive production makes it worth more than gold by weight.

Bread was once used as an eraser.
Before modern erasers, people used moistened bread to remove pencil marks from paper.

Cashews grow on the bottom of a fruit.
The cashew nut is actually a seed that grows beneath the cashew apple, which is often discarded or used to make juice.

The Aztecs invented guacamole.
They called it *ahuacamolli,* which translates to "avocado sauce," and used it as a staple in their diet.

Bread was used as a plate in medieval times.
Known as "trenchers," thick slices of stale bread served as edible plates for meals.

Tomatoes were once called "love apples."
In the 16th century, Europeans believed tomatoes were an aphrodisiac and nicknamed them accordingly.

Ice cream sundaes were created to avoid Sunday laws.
Blue laws prohibited selling soda on Sundays, so soda fountains served ice cream with syrup instead, creating the sundae.

Cinnamon comes from tree bark.
This popular spice is made by drying and curling the inner bark of cinnamon trees.

There's a fruit that smells like rotting garbage but tastes amazing.
Durian, known as the "king of fruits," has a notoriously pungent smell but a sweet and creamy flavor.

Soy sauce can take up to two years to brew.
Traditional soy sauce is fermented for months, or even years, to develop its rich flavor.

Caramel was invented by accident.
Sugar workers in ancient Persia discovered caramel while trying to create hard candy, accidentally burning the sugar.

The most expensive steak costs over $1,000.
Japanese Wagyu beef, especially A5-grade Kobe, is prized for its marbling and tenderness, commanding a hefty price tag.

Almonds are seeds, not nuts.
Almonds are the seeds of the almond tree's fruit, which resembles a peach.

Margarine was created as a cheap butter substitute.
Invented in 1869 by Hippolyte Mège-Mouriès, margarine was developed for French soldiers as an affordable alternative to butter.

Vanilla ice cream was originally black.
The first vanilla ice cream used unprocessed vanilla beans, which turned the mixture black instead of white.

Caviar was once a poor man's food.
In 19th-century Russia, sturgeon roe was so abundant it was given away for free in taverns.

Chocolate was originally consumed as a drink.
The ancient Mayans and Aztecs drank cacao as a bitter beverage mixed with spices, not the sweet treat we know today.

You can make wine from bananas.
Banana wine is a popular alcoholic beverage in parts of Africa and the Caribbean, made by fermenting bananas with sugar.

Potatoes contain a small amount of poison.
Green potatoes and their sprouts contain solanine, a toxin that can cause nausea if consumed in large amounts.

There's a mushroom that tastes like fried chicken.
Laetiporus, also known as "chicken of the woods," is a wild fungus with a texture and flavor similar to chicken.

The color of a bell pepper indicates its ripeness.
Green peppers are unripe, while yellow, orange, and red peppers represent different stages of maturity.

One pound of saffron requires 75,000 flowers.
Each flower of the crocus plant produces only three strands of saffron, making it incredibly labor-intensive to harvest.

Peppers were named after black pepper.
When Europeans discovered chili peppers, they mistakenly thought they were related to black pepper and gave them the same name.

Instant ramen was invented during a food shortage.
In post-World War II Japan, Momofuku Ando created instant noodles as a cheap and long-lasting meal option.

Sugar can heal wounds.
Granulated sugar, when applied to wounds, helps kill bacteria by drawing out moisture, speeding up healing.

The "white stuff" on chocolate isn't mold.
It's called chocolate bloom, a harmless result of fat or sugar separating due to temperature changes.

Coconut water can be used as IV fluid.
During World War II, doctors used sterile coconut water as a blood plasma substitute in emergencies.

There's a fruit that explodes when ripe.
The sandbox tree produces exploding fruit that bursts open to spread its seeds, earning it the nickname "dynamite tree."

Soybeans can be made into everything from milk to meat substitutes.
This versatile legume is a staple in plant-based diets, providing protein in countless forms.

Pineapples regenerate themselves.
Once harvested, the pineapple plant can regrow from its crown, producing another fruit in about two years.

Melted cheese was a medieval delicacy.
Fondue, originally a simple dish for Swiss peasants, became a luxurious way to enjoy stale bread and cheese.

White chocolate isn't actually chocolate.
It contains no cocoa solids, only cocoa butter, sugar, and milk, which is why it tastes so different.

Chopsticks were originally cooking utensils.
Invented over 3,000 years ago in China, chopsticks were first used for stirring and serving hot food.

The Caesar salad originated in Mexico.
Created by Italian-American restaurateur Caesar Cardini in Tijuana, the salad became a global classic.

There's a type of coffee bean that sinks instead of floats.
Peaberry coffee beans are denser than regular beans, which makes them sink in water tests.

Apples float because they're 25% air.
Their cellular structure traps air pockets, making them buoyant enough for bobbing contests.

Chewing gum burns calories.
Although minimal, chewing gum can burn about 11 calories per hour.

Baking powder was invented in 1843.
Alfred Bird created it for his wife, who was allergic to yeast, revolutionizing baking.

Champagne can only be called Champagne if it's from France.
By law, sparkling wine must come from the Champagne region and follow strict production rules to bear the name.

Some cheese is aged in caves.
Varieties like Roquefort and Gouda are aged in caves to develop unique flavors and textures.

Milk was once used as glue.
Casein, a protein in milk, was used to create adhesives before synthetic glues were developed.

Pop rocks were discovered by accident.
Chemist William Mitchell created the fizzy candy while attempting to invent an instant soda.

Almond milk was popular in medieval times.
Before refrigeration, almond milk was a shelf-stable alternative to cow's milk.

Grapes explode in the microwave.
When microwaved, grapes create plasma arcs, causing them to spark and sometimes explode.

Fortune cookies are not Chinese.
They were invented in California in the early 20th century and popularized in American-Chinese restaurants.

There's a cheese that smells like feet but tastes amazing.
Limburger cheese has a pungent aroma but a mild, creamy flavor that pairs well with bread and onions.

The world's largest wine barrel holds 58,000 gallons.
Located in Germany, this colossal barrel is an engineering marvel—and completely empty.

A tomato is both a fruit and a vegetable.
Botanically, it's a fruit, but legally, it's a vegetable, thanks to an 1893 U.S. Supreme Court ruling.

Broccoli is a man-made vegetable.
Developed from wild cabbage through selective breeding, broccoli is entirely a human invention.

Bread can predict the weather.
In medieval times, people used how bread dough rose to predict humidity levels and impending rain.

Black pepper was once called "black gold."
Highly prized in ancient times, it was used as currency and was a significant driver of global trade.

You can eat banana peels.
While most people discard them, banana peels are edible, packed with nutrients, and often used in vegan recipes.

Salt was once used as currency.
In ancient Rome, soldiers were partially paid in salt, which is where the word "salary" originates.

There's a fruit that tastes like meat.
Jackfruit, native to Southeast Asia, has a texture and flavor similar to pulled pork when cooked.

There's gold in some drinks.
Goldschläger, a cinnamon schnapps, contains real gold flakes, which are safe to consume.

You can make plastic from milk.
Casein, a protein in milk, can be used to create a biodegradable plastic known as "milk plastic."

Eggs have thousands of tiny pores.
A single eggshell can have up to 17,000 microscopic pores, allowing gases to pass through.

Chili peppers trick your brain into feeling heat.
Capsaicin binds to pain receptors in your mouth, simulating the sensation of burning without actual heat.

The most expensive water costs $60,000.
Acqua di Cristallo Tributo a Modigliani comes in a gold bottle and is sourced from exotic springs worldwide.

Garlic was once believed to ward off evil spirits.
Used in folklore and mythology, garlic was thought to protect against vampires and other supernatural threats.

Sugar was used to clean wounds.
Before antibiotics, granulated sugar was sprinkled on wounds to prevent infection and promote healing.

Worcestershire sauce contains fermented fish.
This iconic condiment is made with anchovies that are fermented in vinegar for up to two years.

Coconuts kill more people than sharks.
Falling coconuts cause around 150 deaths annually, far surpassing shark-related fatalities.

BIZARRE LAWS AND CUSTOMS

Strange traditions, laws, and practices from around the world.

In France, it's illegal to name a pig "Napoleon."
A law was passed to protect the dignity of France's famous leader, forbidding his name from being used for swine.

In Switzerland, flushing the toilet after 10 PM is illegal in some apartments.
This noise ordinance is meant to reduce disturbances in multi-family housing units.

In Venice, feeding pigeons is against the law.
To preserve its historic buildings, Venice banned feeding pigeons in 2008, as their droppings damage stonework.

In Samoa, it's a crime to forget your wife's birthday.
If you miss your spouse's special day, you could face fines or public shaming.

Chewing gum is banned in Singapore.
To keep public spaces clean, Singapore outlawed gum in 1992, except for medicinal purposes.

In Japan, slurping noodles is considered polite.
While it might seem rude elsewhere, slurping loudly shows you're enjoying your meal in Japan.

In Thailand, it's illegal to step on money.
Thai currency features the king's image, and stepping on it is considered disrespectful and a punishable offense.

In England, it's illegal to handle salmon suspiciously.
Under the Salmon Act of 1986, suspicious handling of salmon can lead to legal consequences.

In Germany, running out of gas on the Autobahn is illegal.
Drivers are expected to keep their cars fueled, as stopping on the high-speed road is dangerous and prohibited.

In Australia, it's illegal to disrupt a wedding.
Interrupting a wedding ceremony can lead to fines or even jail time under Australian law.

In Scotland, it's a legal requirement to let someone use your bathroom.
If someone knocks on your door and asks to use the toilet, you're legally obligated to let them in.

In China, reincarnation requires government approval.
Tibetan Buddhist monks must get permission from the Chinese government before being reincarnated.

In Canada, it's illegal to pretend to practice witchcraft.
Falsely claiming to perform witchcraft can land you in trouble, though practicing it sincerely is allowed.

In Milan, it's a law to smile at all times.
Except at funerals or hospitals, residents are legally obligated to smile, reflecting the city's cheerful spirit.

In Denmark, naming your child is highly regulated.
Parents must choose from an approved list of names or seek government approval for unique ones.

In Portugal, it's illegal to pee in the ocean.
Though enforcement might be tricky, this law exists to maintain water cleanliness.

In New Zealand, flying with a rooster is prohibited.
Roosters are banned from airplanes due to their potential to disrupt the peace with crowing.

In Alabama, it's illegal to wear a fake mustache in church.
If the mustache causes laughter, you could face a fine for disrupting the service.

In Italy, it's illegal to die in certain towns.
Places like Falciano del Massico have banned death due to overcrowded cemeteries, a tongue-in-cheek way to draw attention to the issue.

In India, cow crimes are taken seriously.
Harming a cow, considered sacred in Hinduism, can result in jail time or hefty fines.

In South Korea, tipping is considered rude.
Unlike in many countries, tipping is not customary, and attempting to tip might confuse or offend locals.

In Florida, it's illegal to pass gas in public after 6 PM.
This outdated law was meant to reduce disturbances during evening hours, though enforcement is nonexistent.

In Japan, tattoos can limit public access.
Many traditional bathhouses and swimming pools ban tattoos due to their association with organized crime.

In the UK, it's illegal to handle a fish suspiciously.
Under the Fraud Act of 2006, carrying fish in a strange manner can raise legal questions.

In Iceland, you must get government approval to name your child.
The Icelandic Naming Committee ensures names fit grammar and tradition before granting approval.

In France, it's illegal to take a photo of the Eiffel Tower at night.
The tower's nighttime light display is copyrighted, making sharing those photos technically illegal without permission.

In Norway, knocking on someone's door and running away is illegal.
Known as "knock-and-run," this prank is punishable by fines if reported to the authorities.

In Vermont, women need permission to wear false teeth.
A law requires a woman to get written consent from her husband before obtaining dentures.

In South Africa, it's illegal to sit closer than two meters to a giraffe.
This regulation is meant to ensure the safety of both humans and the animals.

In Greece, wearing high heels at archaeological sites is banned.
To protect ancient ruins, visitors are prohibited from wearing shoes that might cause damage.

In Switzerland, owning only one guinea pig is illegal.
Because guinea pigs are social animals, Swiss law requires you to have at least two to prevent loneliness.

In Bhutan, wearing traditional dress is mandatory in public.
Bhutanese citizens must wear their national attire, *gho* for men and *kira* for women, in formal settings and public offices.

In Samoa, it's illegal to forget to attend church.
Regular church attendance is taken seriously, and missing a service can lead to fines.

In Spain, it's illegal to drive in flip-flops.
This footwear is considered unsafe for driving, and violators can be fined.

In the Maldives, public displays of affection are banned.
As a conservative Muslim country, hugging or kissing in public can result in fines or imprisonment.

In Russia, driving a dirty car is illegal.
If your license plate or car body is deemed too dirty, you could be fined by authorities.

In Thailand, it's illegal to leave your house without underwear.
This little-known law exists but is rarely enforced.

In South Africa, wrestling a bear is illegal.
Though bears aren't native to the region, the law forbids importing them for fights or performances.

In the UK, it's illegal to use a phone to pay at a drive-thru.
Because using your phone while the car is running counts as operating a vehicle, it's technically against the law.

In North Korea, blue jeans are banned.
Considered a symbol of Western influence, wearing denim is strictly prohibited.

In Canada, it's illegal to scare a child to death.
Laws against creating life-threatening fear protect minors from excessive pranks or threats.

In the UAE, swearing on WhatsApp is punishable by fines.
Even private messages are subject to cybercrime laws, and profanity can lead to penalties.

In India, playing the national anthem in a movie theater is mandatory.
Before a film begins, theaters play the anthem, and patrons are required to stand.

In Italy, goldfish bowls are banned.
To promote animal welfare, spherical fish bowls, which distort vision and reduce oxygen, are prohibited.

In Sweden, naming your child "Ikea" is illegal.
The country has strict naming laws, and using the furniture giant's name is not allowed.

In France, it's illegal to kiss on train platforms.
This law was introduced in 1910 to prevent train delays caused by long goodbyes.

In Japan, eating while walking is frowned upon.
While not illegal, it's considered impolite to eat on the go, as meals should be enjoyed while seated.

In Mexico, wearing high heels in certain towns is illegal.
To prevent damage to cobblestone streets, some municipalities have banned high-heeled shoes in historic areas.

In Oklahoma, it's illegal to make ugly faces at a dog.
This quirky law aims to prevent animal cruelty, even if it's just through expressions.

In Finland, speeding tickets are based on income.
Wealthier individuals pay more for speeding violations, making the punishment proportional to their earnings.

In Texas, it's illegal to sell your eyeballs.
Selling body parts, including your eyeballs, is strictly prohibited in the Lone Star State.

In Japan, drivers who splash pedestrians can be fined.
If you drench someone while driving through a puddle, you could face a hefty fine for your lack of consideration.

In Singapore, not flushing the toilet is illegal.
Public restrooms are monitored, and failure to flush can result in a fine.

In China, you can be fined for reincarnating without permission.
Buddhist monks are required to seek government approval before being reincarnated.

In Kentucky, you can't dye a duckling blue and sell it.
Unless you're selling at least six dyed animals at once, it's against the law to color them.

In Germany, pillows are considered weapons.
In certain cases, hitting someone with a pillow can be classified as assault under German law.

In Arizona, it's illegal to let a donkey sleep in a bathtub.
This law was passed after a flood carried a donkey in a bathtub downstream, causing a costly rescue operation.

In South Carolina, it's illegal to seduce an unmarried woman.
This outdated law is still technically on the books, though rarely enforced.

In Turkey, you must carry your ID at all times.
Failing to produce identification upon request can lead to fines or detention.

In the Philippines, smiling is mandatory in certain cities.
A "Smile Policy" in cities like Bacolod requires residents to greet others with a smile to promote happiness.

In Canada, you can't pay with more than 25 cents in pennies.
To prevent inconvenience, there are legal limits on how much you can pay using coins.

In Italy, sand theft is a serious crime.
Taking sand or pebbles from beaches can result in fines of up to €3,000 to protect the environment.

In Israel, picking flowers from national parks is illegal.
Even if the flowers seem abundant, plucking them can lead to steep fines.

In Greece, men are required to wear pants in certain public places.
This law exists to maintain decorum, particularly in historic or religious sites.

In Iceland, you can't own a pet snake.
Exotic pets like snakes, lizards, and turtles are banned to protect local ecosystems.

In Russia, you can be fined for driving a dirty car.
If your car is excessively dirty, especially the license plate, you risk a ticket from traffic authorities.

In Spain, building sandcastles is banned in some regions.
Certain beaches prohibit sandcastle-building to maintain their natural beauty and avoid overcrowding.

In Hungary, whistling indoors is considered bad luck.
Locals believe it invites financial misfortune or spirits into the home.

In France, men must wear Speedos at public pools.
Loose-fitting swim trunks are banned to ensure hygiene standards.

In Thailand, driving shirtless is illegal.
Drivers are required to wear a shirt while operating a vehicle, even in the sweltering heat.

In Denmark, you must check for children under your car.
Drivers are legally obligated to inspect their vehicle for hidden children before driving away.

In Switzerland, mowing your lawn on Sundays is frowned upon.
Lawn mowing is considered a noisy disturbance, and Sunday is reserved for peace and quiet.

In Norway, it's illegal to spay or neuter your pet without a valid reason.
The government promotes natural animal behaviors unless health concerns
necessitate sterilization.

In China, you can't use reincarnation without approval.
Monks seeking to reincarnate must first gain government consent, even for spiritual
matters.

In Finland, a taxi driver must pay music royalties.
If they play music for passengers, taxi drivers are required to pay fees to music
licensing organizations.

In Australia, it's illegal to walk on the right side of the road.
Pedestrians are required to walk on the left to avoid collisions with oncoming traffic.

In Alabama, playing dominoes on Sundays is illegal.
This outdated law was originally intended to discourage gambling on the Sabbath.

In Japan, taking food from a friend's plate is considered bad manners.
This practice is frowned upon as sharing is reserved for specific customs, like giving
sushi with chopsticks.

In the UK, it's illegal to wear armor in Parliament.
A law from 1313 prohibits wearing armor in the House of Commons or House of
Lords.

In Texas, you can't milk someone else's cow.
Unauthorized milking is considered theft under state law.

In Canada, dragging a dead horse down the street is illegal.
This archaic law was created to keep public roads clean.

In France, dogs can inherit money.
French law allows pets to be named as beneficiaries in wills, often handled through trusts.

In Vermont, it's illegal to whistle underwater.
While enforcement is unlikely, this quirky law exists in the state's legal code.

In South Korea, red ink is bad luck.
Writing someone's name in red ink is considered a death omen, so it's avoided at all costs.

In Japan, overweight people are monitored by law.
The "Metabo Law" requires citizens to maintain waist measurements below specific thresholds.

In India, cows have right of way on roads.
Cows, considered sacred, are free to roam streets, and drivers must wait for them to move.

In California, you can't peel an orange in a hotel room.
This strange law was intended to prevent citrus scents from lingering in shared spaces.

In Russia, no selfies in dangerous places.
Selfies near cliffs, rooftops, or railways are banned to reduce accidental deaths.

In Thailand, stepping on money is illegal.
Stepping on currency is considered an insult to the monarchy, as Thai bills feature the king's image.

In Switzerland, owning a single guinea pig is illegal.
Guinea pigs are social animals, so Swiss law requires you to have at least two to prevent loneliness.

In Poland, wearing Winnie the Pooh shirts is banned in some areas.
Pooh's lack of pants is considered inappropriate for children in playgrounds and schools.

In Hawaii, billboards are banned.
To preserve natural beauty, Hawaii prohibits most outdoor advertising, making it the only U.S. state without billboards.

In Italy, it's illegal to have goldfish in a round bowl.
Round fishbowls are thought to cause poor oxygenation and distorted vision, harming the fish.

In France, you must carry a breathalyzer in your car.
Drivers are required to have a portable breathalyzer kit available, though enforcement is rare.

In Spain, eating on public transportation is banned.
This law exists to keep buses and trains clean for all passengers.

In Germany, running out of gas on the Autobahn is illegal.
Stopping unnecessarily is forbidden on the high-speed highway for safety reasons.

In Norway, naming your child "Devil" is banned.
Certain names are prohibited to protect children from embarrassment or harm.

In South Africa, giraffes have right of way.
Drivers must yield to these towering animals, even if it causes traffic delays.

In Japan, it's illegal to litter near Mount Fuji.
To preserve the iconic mountain, strict rules prohibit littering in its surrounding areas.

In Sweden, it's illegal to name your child "Elvis."
The Swedish Naming Law prohibits names that could cause discomfort or embarrassment.

In Canada, it's illegal to climb trees in Oshawa.
This city law aims to prevent injuries and damage to public property.

In France, you can marry a dead person.
Posthumous marriage, called *mariage posthume*, is legal under special circumstances with government approval.

In Australia, it's illegal to disrupt a wedding or funeral.
Interfering with these ceremonies can result in fines or imprisonment.

In Japan, dancing after midnight was banned until 2015.
This outdated law, intended to curb crime, was repealed after public outcry.

In the UK, handling a fish suspiciously is illegal.
The Salmon Act of 1986 includes a peculiar clause about handling fish in unusual ways.

In Switzerland, it's illegal to own just one parrot.
Parrots are social creatures, and Swiss law requires owners to keep them in pairs.

In the UAE, swearing on social media can result in fines.
Even private messages are subject to cybercrime laws, with penalties including imprisonment.

In Germany, it's illegal to tune your piano at night.
To maintain peace, piano tuning is prohibited after 10 PM.

In Samoa, it's illegal to forget to attend church.
Missing Sunday services can result in public shaming or fines in some communities.

In Russia, lace underwear is banned.
A law requires clothing, including underwear, to meet a specific minimum cotton content for safety and hygiene.

In South Korea, there's a curfew on gaming for children.
Known as the "Cinderella Law," minors under 16 cannot play online games between midnight and 6 AM.

In Thailand, it's illegal to leave your house without underwear.
While rarely enforced, this law exists as part of the country's decency regulations.

In Singapore, spitting in public is illegal.
This law aims to keep the city clean, with hefty fines for offenders.

In Italy, men are banned from wearing skirts.
Cross-dressing laws, though rarely enforced, exist in certain conservative regions.

In Greece, high heels are banned at ancient sites.
To protect historic ruins, visitors must wear flat shoes.

In Japan, tattoos can limit access to public baths.
Tattooed individuals are often barred from bathhouses due to their association with organized crime.

In California, eating oranges in the bathtub is illegal.
This bizarre law was reportedly created to prevent plumbing issues caused by citrus oils.

In Scotland, it's illegal to be drunk in charge of a cow.
Drunken cow-herding could result in fines or imprisonment under an old law.

In Spain, driving while wearing flip-flops is illegal.
This footwear is considered unsafe for driving and can result in fines if caught.

In France, you cannot disinherit your children.
French inheritance laws ensure that children receive a guaranteed portion of their parent's estate.

In Alaska, waking a bear to take a photo is illegal.
This law protects both bears and tourists from dangerous encounters.

In India, it's illegal to export cows.
Since cows are sacred in Hinduism, exporting them for slaughter is strictly prohibited.

In Norway, it's illegal to advertise to children under 12.
This consumer protection law ensures children aren't targeted by marketing campaigns.

In Thailand, littering on the beach can result in jail time.
Fines and imprisonment aim to preserve the country's pristine coastal areas.

In Switzerland, flushing toilets at night is banned in apartments.
This law prevents noise disturbances in multi-family housing units.

In Mexico, you can't whistle at women.
Catcalling is considered harassment and can lead to legal consequences.

In Russia, driving a dirty car can result in a fine.
Authorities may ticket drivers if their license plate or car body is excessively dirty.

In North Korea, blue jeans are banned.
Denim is seen as a symbol of Western influence and is prohibited under strict dress codes.

UNSOLVED MYSTERIES

Mysteries and enigmas that continue to baffle humanity.

The Disappearance of the Roanoke Colony
In 1587, over 100 settlers vanished from Roanoke Island, leaving only the cryptic word "CROATOAN" carved into a tree. Their fate remains unknown.

The Voynich Manuscript
This 600-year-old book is written in an unknown language and features bizarre illustrations of plants, astrological symbols, and bathing women. Despite numerous attempts, it has never been fully decoded.

The Bermuda Triangle
A region in the North Atlantic Ocean is infamous for unexplained disappearances of ships and aircraft. No definitive scientific explanation has been found.

The Mary Celeste
In 1872, this American merchant ship was found adrift in the Atlantic Ocean, fully stocked and undamaged, but without a single crew member aboard.

The Zodiac Killer
This infamous serial killer terrorized Northern California in the 1960s and 1970s, sending cryptic letters to newspapers. His identity remains unknown.

The Dyatlov Pass Incident
In 1959, nine Russian hikers died under mysterious circumstances in the Ural Mountains, with injuries ranging from fractured skulls to missing eyes. Theories range from avalanches to alien encounters.

Jack the Ripper
In 1888, a killer stalked London's Whitechapel district, murdering at least five women. Despite extensive investigations, his identity remains a mystery.

The Taos Hum
Residents of Taos, New Mexico, report hearing a low-frequency hum with no identifiable source. Scientists have been unable to pinpoint the cause.

The Lost City of Atlantis
First described by Plato, the advanced civilization of Atlantis supposedly sank into the ocean. Its existence has never been proven.

The Green Children of Woolpit
In 12th-century England, two children with green skin appeared in the village of Woolpit. They spoke an unknown language and claimed to be from an underground world.

The Black Dahlia Murder
In 1947, aspiring actress Elizabeth Short was found murdered in Los Angeles, her body gruesomely mutilated. The case remains unsolved.

The Somerton Man
In 1948, an unidentified man was found dead on Somerton Beach in Australia, with a scrap of paper reading "Tamam Shud" in his pocket. The case has baffled investigators for decades.

The Wow! Signal
A mysterious space signal detected in 1977 has yet to be explained. Was it aliens, a cosmic anomaly, or something else entirely?

The Curse of Oak Island
For over 200 years, treasure hunters have searched for riches supposedly hidden on Oak Island in Nova Scotia. Traps and unexplained phenomena have thwarted every expedition.

The Dancing Plague of 1518
In Strasbourg, France, dozens of people danced uncontrollably for days, with some reportedly dying from exhaustion. No one knows what caused it.

The Tunguska Event
In 1908, a massive explosion flattened 800 square miles of Siberian forest. The leading theory is a meteorite, but no impact crater has ever been found.

The Bloop

A powerful underwater sound detected in 1997 in the Pacific Ocean was initially thought to be from a massive sea creature. It's now attributed to ice movements, but not everyone is convinced.

The Pollock Twins

Two sisters born in 1958 in England seemed to possess memories and behaviors of their deceased siblings, sparking theories of reincarnation.

The Disappearance of Flight MH370

In 2014, Malaysia Airlines Flight 370 vanished with 239 people on board. Despite extensive searches, the plane's exact location remains unknown.

The Phaistos Disc

Discovered in Crete in 1908, this clay disc features mysterious symbols arranged in a spiral. Its purpose and meaning are still undeciphered.

The Lead Masks Case

In 1966, two men in Brazil were found dead wearing lead masks, with no signs of struggle. A cryptic note found nearby has yet to be explained.

The Rendlesham Forest Incident

Often called "Britain's Roswell," this 1980 UFO sighting involved military personnel and unexplained lights near a Suffolk airbase.

The Lizard Man of Scape Ore Swamp

In the 1980s, multiple sightings of a reptilian humanoid in South Carolina sparked widespread curiosity and fear. Its existence remains unproven.

The Hinterkaifeck Murders
In 1922, six people were brutally murdered on a German farmstead. Despite numerous suspects and theories, the case remains unsolved.

The Chupacabra
First reported in Puerto Rico in the 1990s, this cryptid allegedly kills livestock and drinks their blood. Sightings have been reported across the Americas.

The Lost Treasure of the Flor de la Mar
This 16th-century Portuguese ship sank off the coast of Sumatra, carrying a massive fortune. Despite numerous expeditions, the treasure remains missing.

The MV Joyita
In 1955, this merchant vessel was found drifting in the Pacific Ocean with no crew on board. The circumstances of their disappearance remain a mystery.

The Babushka Lady
A woman seen filming during JFK's assassination has never been identified, and her footage has never surfaced.

The Isdal Woman
In 1970, the charred body of an unidentified woman was found in Norway's Isdalen Valley, surrounded by cryptic clues. Her identity and cause of death remain unknown.

The Green Fireballs
In the late 1940s, glowing green orbs were frequently spotted in the skies over New Mexico. Their origin remains unexplained.

The Ghost Ship Mary Celeste
Found adrift in 1872, this ship was intact and fully stocked, but the crew had
vanished without a trace.

The Disappearance of Amelia Earhart
In 1937, Earhart vanished during an attempt to circumnavigate the globe. Theories
range from a crash at sea to capture by enemy forces.

The Disappearance of Percy Fawcett
In 1925, explorer Percy Fawcett vanished in the Amazon while searching for the
mythical "City of Z." Neither he nor his expedition was ever found.

The Phoenix Lights
In 1997, thousands of people in Arizona witnessed a series of unexplained lights in
the night sky. The event remains one of the most well-documented UFO sightings.

The Zodiac Killer's Ciphers
Despite one being cracked in 2020, several cryptic messages from the Zodiac Killer
remain undeciphered, possibly holding clues to his identity.

The Disappearance of Jimmy Hoffa
The labor union leader vanished in 1975, and despite countless theories involving
the mob and political rivals, his fate remains unknown.

The Yuba County Five
In 1978, five men disappeared in the Sierra Nevada Mountains. Four were later
found dead, but the fifth was never located, leaving more questions than answers.

The Vanishing Village of Angikuni Lake
A remote Inuit village in Canada was reportedly found abandoned in the 1930s, with no trace of its residents or explanation for their disappearance.

The Hollinwell Incident
In 1980, over 300 people, mostly children, collapsed at a marching band competition in England. The cause of the mass fainting remains unexplained.

The Max Headroom Incident
In 1987, a mysterious hacker wearing a Max Headroom mask hijacked two Chicago TV stations, broadcasting cryptic and bizarre messages. The culprit was never caught.

The Disappearance of the Sodder Children
In 1945, five children disappeared after a house fire in West Virginia. The family suspected they were kidnapped, but no evidence surfaced.

The Silent Twins
June and Jennifer Gibbons, who communicated only with each other, developed a mysterious connection. Jennifer died under strange circumstances in 1993, leaving their bond unexplained.

The Death Valley Germans
In 1996, a family of four went missing in Death Valley National Park. Despite partial remains being found years later, the details of their demise are still unclear.

The Men in Black
Numerous witnesses claim to have been visited by mysterious, black-suited men after UFO sightings, raising questions about their identity and purpose.

The Devil's Footprints
In 1855, a trail of hoof-like prints appeared in the snow across 100 miles in Devon, England. Their origin remains unknown.

The Flannan Isles Lighthouse Mystery
In 1900, three lighthouse keepers vanished from the remote Flannan Isles. Their disappearance has never been explained.

The Tunguska Explosion
A massive explosion in Siberia in 1908 flattened 800 square miles of forest. No impact crater was found, and its cause is still debated.

The Monster with 21 Faces
A criminal group in Japan taunted police and corporations with threats and extortion in the 1980s, but they were never caught.

The Hessdalen Lights
Strange lights in the Hessdalen Valley in Norway have been reported since the 1930s, with no definitive explanation for their source.

The Stone Spheres of Costa Rica
Hundreds of perfectly round stone spheres, some weighing tons, were discovered in the jungle. Their purpose and creators remain a mystery.

The Vanishing of Lars Mittank
In 2014, a German tourist fled an airport in Bulgaria under strange circumstances and was never seen again.

The Chicago Tylenol Murders
In 1982, several people died after consuming Tylenol laced with cyanide. The perpetrator was never identified.

The Khamar-Daban Incident
In 1993, six hikers died mysteriously in Siberia under circumstances similar to the Dyatlov Pass Incident.

The Death of Elisa Lam
In 2013, Elisa Lam was found dead in a water tank at Los Angeles' Cecil Hotel. Her bizarre elevator behavior and the lack of foul play remain unexplained.

The Disappearance of Emanuela Orlandi
This 15-year-old Vatican City resident disappeared in 1983. Her case has been linked to conspiracy theories involving the Vatican and organized crime.

The Black Knight Satellite
Conspiracy theorists believe a mysterious object orbiting Earth, detected in the 1960s, is of alien origin. NASA says it's likely space debris.

The Circleville Letters
In the 1970s and 80s, anonymous threatening letters plagued an Ohio town. Despite a suspect being jailed, the letters continued, and the writer's identity is still unknown.

The Lost Treasure of Montezuma
The Aztec emperor's vast wealth vanished after the Spanish conquest, and its location has never been found.

The Betz Sphere
In 1974, the Betz family discovered a mysterious metallic sphere that exhibited strange behaviors, including moving on its own. Its origin remains unknown.

The Babushka Lady
This unidentified woman was seen filming during JFK's assassination, but her footage has never been found, and her identity remains a mystery.

The Mothman of Point Pleasant
Between 1966 and 1967, sightings of a winged humanoid creature terrified residents of West Virginia. Its purpose and origin remain unexplained.

The Phaistos Disc
This ancient clay disc, discovered in Crete, is covered in mysterious symbols that archaeologists have yet to decipher.

The Eilean Mor Lighthouse Mystery
In 1900, three lighthouse keepers disappeared from the Scottish island, leaving behind untouched meals and a log describing storms that never occurred.

The Marree Man
In 1998, a massive geoglyph of an Aboriginal hunter appeared in the Australian outback. Its creator has never come forward.

The Great Amherst Mystery
In the 1870s, a Canadian house was plagued by violent poltergeist activity, including spontaneous fires and moving objects, that was never explained.

The Disappearance of Harold Holt

Australia's prime minister vanished while swimming in 1967. His body was never recovered, sparking theories ranging from drowning to defection.

The Utsuro-Bune Incident

In 1803, Japanese villagers reportedly found a strange woman in a UFO-like vessel washed ashore. Her origin and fate are unknown.

The Kaspar Hauser Enigma

In 1828, a young man appeared in Germany claiming to have been raised in isolation. His identity and mysterious death remain unsolved.

The Cryptos Sculpture at CIA Headquarters

This cryptographic sculpture features four encrypted messages, three of which have been solved. The fourth remains a mystery.

The Disappearance of the Beaumont Children

In 1966, three siblings vanished from a beach in Adelaide, Australia, sparking one of the country's largest-ever manhunts. They were never found.

The Vanishing of DB Cooper

In 1971, a man hijacked a plane, parachuted out with $200,000 in ransom money, and disappeared without a trace.

The Disappearance of Glenn Miller

In 1944, the famous musician's plane vanished over the English Channel. Neither the wreckage nor his body has ever been recovered.

The Whitechapel Bell Foundry Mystery
This London factory, where Big Ben and the Liberty Bell were cast, closed abruptly in 2017, leaving unanswered questions about its future and legacy.

The Death of Edgar Allan Poe
The famous writer was found delirious on the streets of Baltimore in 1849, wearing someone else's clothes. The cause of his death remains unknown.

The Lost Colony of Greenland Vikings
The Norse settlers in Greenland disappeared around the 15th century. Whether they perished, emigrated, or were assimilated by native populations is unknown.

The Texarkana Moonlight Murders
In 1946, a masked serial killer attacked eight people in Texas. The case inspired the film *The Town That Dreaded Sundown* but remains unsolved.

The Mystery of the Green Children of Woolpit
Two children with green skin appeared in an English village in the 12th century. They claimed to come from a subterranean world.

The Vanishing of Frederick Valentich
In 1978, a pilot disappeared while flying over Australia's Bass Strait. His last radio transmission described an unidentified flying object.

The Black Knight Satellite
Some conspiracy theorists claim an alien satellite has been orbiting Earth for 13,000 years. NASA attributes it to space debris, but speculation persists.

The Missing Sodder Children
In 1945, a fire destroyed the Sodder family home in West Virginia. Five of the ten children were never found, leading to theories of kidnapping.

The Circleville Letters
An anonymous letter-writer terrorized an Ohio town in the 1970s and 1980s, even after the prime suspect was jailed.

The Voynich Manuscript Plants
This ancient text contains illustrations of plants that don't resemble any known species, adding to its mystery.

The Isdal Woman
In 1970, a woman's charred body was found in Norway's Isdalen Valley, surrounded by coded messages and disguises. Her identity remains a mystery.

The Vanishing Village of Angikuni Lake
In the 1930s, an entire Inuit village in Canada reportedly disappeared without a trace, leaving food and belongings behind.

The Hum
A low-frequency hum, heard in places like Taos, New Mexico, and Bristol, England, has no known source. Only certain people can hear it.

The Tunguska Trees
Trees near the site of the 1908 Siberian explosion grew faster than normal afterward, leading to speculation about the event's cause.

The Dyatlov Tent
When discovered, the hikers' tent in the Dyatlov Pass incident was bizarrely torn open from the inside, adding to the mystery.

The Vanishing Lighthouse Keepers of Eilean Mor
In 1900, three Scottish lighthouse keepers disappeared, leaving behind untouched meals and a log describing a mysterious storm.

The Cursed Treasure of Oak Island
For centuries, treasure hunters have searched Oak Island in Nova Scotia for buried riches, only to encounter deadly traps and dead ends.

The Missing Roanoke Carving
The word "CROATOAN" was carved into a tree at the abandoned Roanoke Colony. Its meaning has never been fully understood.

The Marree Man
A massive geoglyph of an Aboriginal hunter appeared in the Australian outback in 1998. Its creator has never come forward.

The Ghost Ship Mary Celeste
In 1872, this ship was found adrift in the Atlantic with no one aboard, despite being fully stocked and seaworthy.

The Babushka Lady
This woman was seen filming during JFK's assassination, but her footage and identity have never surfaced.

The Silent Twins
June and Jennifer Gibbons, twins from Wales, communicated only with each other and exhibited strange behaviors. Jennifer's sudden death in 1993 remains unexplained.

The Lost Amber Room
A priceless Russian treasure made of amber panels vanished during World War II and has never been recovered.

The Vanishing Crew of the MV Joyita
In 1955, this merchant vessel was found drifting in the Pacific with no crew aboard. The circumstances remain a mystery.

The Monster of Glamis Castle
Legend speaks of a deformed child locked away in Glamis Castle, Scotland. The truth behind the tale is still debated.

The Missing Head of King Badu Bonsu II
The severed head of an African king was taken by the Dutch in the 19th century and lost for over a century before being rediscovered in 2009.

The Death of Bobby Fuller
The musician was found dead in his car in 1966 under suspicious circumstances. His death was ruled accidental, but many believe foul play was involved.

The Khamar-Daban Incident
In 1993, six hikers died mysteriously in Russia, displaying bizarre symptoms like bleeding from the eyes.

The Rendlesham Forest Incident
Often referred to as Britain's Roswell, this 1980 UFO sighting near a military base has never been fully explained.

The Kaspar Hauser Mystery
In 1828, a boy claiming to have been raised in isolation appeared in Germany. His origins and suspicious death remain a mystery.

The Vanishing Army of King Cambyses
In 525 BC, an army of 50,000 soldiers reportedly vanished in the Egyptian desert during a sandstorm. No evidence of their fate has been found.

The Disappearance of Bison Dele
The former NBA star vanished in 2002 while sailing in the Pacific. His brother, suspected of foul play, committed suicide before the case could be solved.

INVENTORS AND INVENTIONS

Weird and unexpected inventions that changed the world.

Alexander Graham Bell invented the telephone by accident.
Bell was attempting to create a device to help the deaf when he stumbled upon the principles of the telephone, changing communication forever.

Thomas Edison didn't invent the light bulb.
While Edison improved the design, the original concept was created by Sir Humphry Davy in 1800, followed by others like Joseph Swan.

The microwave oven was invented thanks to a melted candy bar.
Percy Spencer discovered microwaves' heating power when a chocolate bar melted in his pocket during radar experiments.

The invention of the pacemaker was inspired by a mistake.
Wilson Greatbatch accidentally inserted the wrong resistor into a circuit, leading to the creation of the first implantable pacemaker.

Post-it Notes were invented because of a failure.
Dr. Spencer Silver was trying to create a super-strong adhesive but ended up with one that stuck lightly and could be removed easily.

The inventor of the sewing machine dreamed of the design.
Elias Howe was inspired to create the sewing machine after dreaming of a needle with an eye at the pointed end.

The first computer bug was an actual bug.
In 1947, Grace Hopper and her team found a moth causing malfunctions in the Harvard Mark II computer, coining the term "debugging."

The inventor of the Frisbee was turned into a Frisbee.
Ed Headrick, who perfected the modern Frisbee, had his ashes molded into Frisbees after his death.

Velcro was inspired by burrs.
Engineer George de Mestral noticed how burrs clung to his dog's fur and used the idea to invent Velcro.

The stethoscope was invented because of modesty.
René Laennec created the stethoscope in 1816 because he felt uncomfortable placing his ear on a woman's chest to listen to her heart.

Bubble wrap was originally designed as wallpaper.
Inventors Alfred Fielding and Marc Chavannes were trying to create textured wallpaper when they stumbled upon the idea for bubble wrap.

Popsicles were invented by an 11-year-old.
In 1905, Frank Epperson accidentally left a cup of soda with a stirring stick outside overnight, creating the first frozen treat.

The Eiffel Tower was supposed to be temporary.
Gustave Eiffel intended for his iconic structure to be dismantled after 20 years, but it became a lasting symbol of France.

The Slinky was invented by mistake.
Naval engineer Richard James accidentally knocked a tension spring off a shelf, and it "walked" across the floor, sparking the idea for the toy.

The first webcam was used to monitor coffee.
In 1991, Cambridge University scientists created the first webcam to keep an eye on the coffee pot in their break room.

Coca-Cola was originally a medicine.
Dr. John Stith Pemberton invented Coca-Cola as a cure for headaches and fatigue, using coca leaf extract and kola nuts.

The inventor of the parachute tested it himself.
In 1783, Louis-Sébastien Lenormand jumped from a tree with two umbrellas, proving the concept of a parachute.

The first automobile was powered by steam.
In 1769, Nicolas-Joseph Cugnot built a steam-powered vehicle, predating gasoline-powered cars by over a century.

The inventor of the safety pin sold it for $400.
Walter Hunt patented the safety pin in 1849 and sold the rights to pay off a debt, missing out on future profits.

The creator of the modern bra used handkerchiefs.
Mary Phelps Jacob invented the first modern bra in 1914 by tying two handkerchiefs together with a ribbon.

The thermometer was invented in the 16th century.
Galileo Galilei created the first thermoscope, the precursor to the modern thermometer, in the early 1600s.

The microwave oven was nearly rejected by manufacturers.
When Percy Spencer pitched the idea, many companies thought consumers wouldn't want a device that cooked with "invisible waves."

The zipper took decades to gain popularity.
Though it was invented in 1893, the zipper didn't become widely used until the 1920s when it was marketed for children's clothing.

Toilet paper was patented in 1857.
Joseph Gayetty introduced toilet paper as "Medicated Paper for the Water-Closet," marketed as a health product.

The first artificial heart was made of plastic.
Dr. Paul Winchell created the first artificial heart in 1963, made entirely of synthetic materials.

The windshield wiper was invented by a woman.
Mary Anderson patented the first windshield wiper in 1903 after observing drivers struggling to see in the rain.

The inventor of basketball used a peach basket.
James Naismith nailed a peach basket to a gym balcony to create the first basketball hoop in 1891.

The roller coaster was inspired by mining carts.
LaMarcus Adna Thompson adapted the concept of coal mine carts for the world's first roller coaster in 1884.

The phonograph was Edison's favorite invention.
Of all his creations, Thomas Edison loved the phonograph most, calling it "the child of my brain."

The light bulb wasn't Edison's first invention.
His first patent was for an electric vote recorder, which never gained popularity.

The Segway inventor disappeared mysteriously.
Dean Kamen's Segway partner, Jimi Heselden, tragically died in 2010 after accidentally driving a Segway off a cliff.

The Rubik's Cube was a teaching tool.
Ernő Rubik created the cube in 1974 to help his students understand three-dimensional geometry.

The first alarm clock could only ring at one time.
In 1787, Levi Hutchins created a clock that rang at 4 AM, his preferred waking time, with no option to change it.

The inventor of dynamite regretted his invention.
Alfred Nobel created dynamite for construction but was disheartened by its use in warfare, inspiring the Nobel Peace Prize.

The adhesive bandage (Band-Aid) was invented for love.
Earle Dickson created Band-Aids in 1920 to help his wife, who frequently injured herself while cooking.

The fax machine predates the telephone.
Alexander Bain patented the first fax machine in 1843, decades before Bell invented the telephone.

The first electric toothbrush was invented in 1954.
The Broxodent was developed in Switzerland and marketed as a high-tech solution for oral hygiene.

The popsicle stick was patented in 1924.
The stick used to hold popsicles was a later addition, making it easier to eat frozen treats on the go.

The first patent ever issued in the U.S. was for potash.
In 1790, Samuel Hopkins received Patent No. 1 for a process to make fertilizer from wood ash.

The inventor of the computer mouse never profited from it.
Douglas Engelbart invented the mouse in 1964 but didn't receive royalties because the patent expired before the technology became widespread.

The first video game was created in 1958.
Physicist William Higinbotham developed *Tennis for Two*, a simple game played on an oscilloscope.

The inventor of the Super Soaker was a NASA engineer.
Lonnie Johnson, who worked on spacecraft for NASA, invented the iconic water gun in his spare time.

The inventor of bubble gum was colorblind.
Walter Diemer accidentally created bubble gum in 1928, and since he couldn't distinguish colors well, he made it pink—the only dye he had.

The first vending machine dispensed holy water.
In 1st-century Alexandria, Hero of Alexandria invented a machine that released holy water when a coin was inserted.

The first email was sent in 1971.
Ray Tomlinson sent the first email to himself as a test, inventing the "@" symbol to route messages.

The inventor of the treadmill created it as a punishment.
Sir William Cubitt invented the treadmill in 1818 for prisoners, forcing them to walk for hours as labor.

The Wright brothers' first flight lasted 12 seconds.
In 1903, Orville Wright piloted the *Flyer* for 12 seconds, covering 120 feet and changing transportation forever.

The first successful parachute jump was from a hot air balloon.
André-Jacques Garnerin leapt from 3,200 feet in 1797, using a silk parachute he designed.

The first television remote was connected by a wire.
In 1950, the "Lazy Bones" remote allowed viewers to change channels, but they often tripped over the cord.

The zipper was originally called the "hookless fastener."
Whitcomb Judson's 1893 invention was rebranded as the zipper in 1923 by the B.F. Goodrich Company.

The creator of the World Wide Web refused to patent it.
Tim Berners-Lee believed the internet should remain free for everyone, declining financial gain for his invention.

The first electric vacuum cleaner was horse-drawn.
In 1901, Hubert Cecil Booth's vacuum cleaner was so large it had to be pulled by horses and powered by an engine.

The first airplane autopilot was invented in 1912.
Elmer Sperry's gyroscopic autopilot allowed planes to maintain stable flight without constant human input.

The microwave was almost marketed as a heating pad.
Early testing suggested its potential for soothing muscle pain before its cooking abilities became the focus.

The Polaroid camera developed pictures in under a minute.
Invented by Edwin Land in 1947, Polaroid cameras revolutionized photography with instant prints.

The phonograph was the first device to record sound.
In 1877, Thomas Edison used a tinfoil cylinder to record himself saying "Mary had a little lamb."

The first ATM pin codes were intended to be six digits.
The inventor, John Shepherd-Barron, reduced it to four digits after his wife said six was too hard to remember.

The first bicycle was nicknamed the "hobby horse."
In 1817, Karl von Drais invented the *draisine*, a two-wheeled vehicle propelled by the rider's feet on the ground.

The first electric fan was invented in 1882.
Schuyler Wheeler created the fan, which brought relief to sweltering homes and offices.

The first car radio was introduced in 1930.
Paul and Joseph Galvin's *Motorola* radio made road trips more entertaining.

The first artificial limb was made in 1529.
Ambroise Paré, a French surgeon, crafted a wooden prosthetic leg with movable joints for increased functionality.

The first digital camera had 0.01 megapixels.
Steve Sasson at Kodak invented the first digital camera in 1975, which took 23 seconds to capture a black-and-white image.

The first electric washing machine was patented in 1908.
The *Thor*, invented by Alva J. Fisher, revolutionized household chores.

The first home refrigerator was invented in 1913.
Fred W. Wolf's "Domelre" was the precursor to the modern fridge, bringing convenience to food storage.

The ballpoint pen was banned in schools.
In the 1940s, schools believed ballpoint pens would ruin handwriting by encouraging laziness compared to fountain pens.

The first patent for a typewriter was filed in 1714.
Henry Mill's design laid the groundwork for modern typewriters, though it wasn't widely used for over a century.

The first submarine was powered by human effort.
The *Turtle*, built in 1775, was a one-man submarine propelled by hand-cranked paddles.

The first escalator was installed as an amusement ride.
In 1896, Coney Island featured an escalator to entertain visitors rather than serve a practical purpose.

The invention of dynamite earned a Nobel Prize.
Alfred Nobel's guilt over the destructive power of dynamite led him to establish the Nobel Prizes.

The Frisbee was inspired by pie tins.
College students in the 1940s started throwing Frisbie Pie Company tins for fun, inspiring the modern toy.

The electric guitar was invented in the 1930s.
Les Paul and George Beauchamp independently developed designs that amplified string vibrations electronically.

The first heart transplant occurred in 1967.
Dr. Christiaan Barnard performed the groundbreaking surgery in South Africa, giving hope to future patients.

The first email emoji was sent in 1982.
Scott Fahlman suggested using :-) to indicate jokes in emails, sparking the emoji culture we know today.

The first electric toaster was patented in 1893.
The *Eclipse* toaster was a simple wire rack heated by electricity, paving the way for the modern appliance.

The first solar-powered calculator debuted in 1978.
The Sharp EL-8026 brought eco-friendly innovation to the world of calculators.

The first recorded invention was the wheel.
Dating back to Mesopotamia in 3500 BC, the wheel revolutionized transportation and machinery.

The smartphone camera began as a novelty.
Sharp's J-SH04, released in 2000, was the first phone with a built-in camera, sparking a revolution in mobile photography.

The first robot vacuum was released in 2002.
The Roomba made autonomous cleaning a household reality, combining robotics and practicality.

The first wristwatch was created for a queen.
In 1810, Abraham-Louis Breguet designed a wristwatch for Queen Caroline Murat of Naples, making it a luxury accessory before becoming a practical tool.

The stapler was invented for King Louis XV.
The first known stapler was created in the 18th century, with each staple engraved with the royal insignia.

The first email was sent to test a new system.
In 1971, Ray Tomlinson sent an email to himself as a test, marking the start of modern electronic communication.

The parachute was sketched by Leonardo da Vinci.
Centuries before its invention, da Vinci designed a pyramid-shaped parachute in the late 1400s.

The electric guitar was once banned in churches.
When first introduced, it was considered too loud and inappropriate for sacred settings.

The pocket calculator changed space exploration.
NASA used early portable calculators to make complex calculations during the Apollo missions.

The first patent for a flying car was filed in 1917.
Glenn Curtiss patented the "Autoplane," which combined a car and airplane but never took off commercially.

The can opener was invented 48 years after the can.
Cans were first opened with knives and hammers until Ezra Warner patented the can opener in 1858.

The first traffic light was installed in 1868.
It was manually operated and located in London, featuring gas lamps to signal stop and go.

The airplane was inspired by bicycles.
The Wright brothers applied their knowledge of bicycles to create their first powered flying machine.

The first video camera weighed over 1,000 pounds.
The RCA Photophone from the 1920s required a team to operate and transport it.

The typewriter was first marketed as a tool for the blind.
Christopher Sholes originally pitched the typewriter as a way for blind people to write legibly.

The first ice cream scoop was patented in 1897.
Alfred L. Cralle's design made serving ice cream easier and remains largely unchanged today.

The elevator brake made skyscrapers possible.
Elisha Otis invented the safety brake in 1853, allowing elevators to stop safely if cables broke.

The electric telegraph used pulses to send messages.
Samuel Morse's invention in 1837 revolutionized communication, giving rise to Morse code.

The first practical telephone call was accidental.
When Bell spilled acid, he called for his assistant, inadvertently proving his invention worked.

The dishwasher was invented by a wealthy socialite.
Josephine Cochrane created the first dishwasher in 1886 to prevent servants from chipping her fine china.

The remote control was originally wired.
Zenith's first TV remote in 1950 used a cable, making it more of a tethered controller than the wireless remotes we use today.

The sewing machine caused riots.
When first introduced in the 19th century, tailors feared the machine would take their jobs and protested its use.

The pencil has been around since the 1500s.
Graphite sticks wrapped in string were the first pencils, later improved with wooden casings.

The clock radio debuted in 1940.
James F. Reynolds combined two essential gadgets, allowing people to wake up to music or the news.

The electric fan was inspired by windmills.
Schuyler Wheeler's invention modernized wind power for indoor cooling.

The ballpoint pen was inspired by newspapers.
László Bíró noticed how ink from newspaper presses dried quickly and adapted the idea for writing.

The GPS system was developed for the military.
Originally used to track submarines, GPS became a civilian tool in the 1980s.

The compact disc (CD) was co-invented by Sony and Philips.
Launched in 1982, the CD revolutionized how music was stored and played.

The safety razor made shaving accessible.
King Camp Gillette's invention in 1901 made shaving safer and easier, replacing straight razors.

The electric toothbrush was invented for patients with braces.
In 1954, Swiss inventor Philippe-Guy Woog created the Broxodent to improve dental hygiene for orthodontic patients.

The thermometer was originally a tube of water.
Early thermometers used water before mercury became the standard in the 1700s.

The first ATM was installed in 1967.
Barclays Bank in London introduced the world's first automated teller machine.

The paperclip design hasn't changed in over a century.
Invented in 1899, Johan Vaaler's paperclip remains one of the simplest yet most effective office tools.

The electric drill was invented in 1889.
Arthur Arnot's design made construction faster and safer, becoming a staple tool.

The microwave oven was an accidental discovery.
Percy Spencer found that radar waves melted a chocolate bar in his pocket, leading to the invention.

RECORDS THAT DEFY LOGIC

World records and human feats that seem impossible.

The Longest Time Spent Without Sleep
Randy Gardner stayed awake for 11 days and 25 minutes in 1964 during a science fair experiment. Surprisingly, he suffered no long-term health issues, though he experienced severe mental impairment.

The Tallest Building Built in Just 19 Days
The Mini Sky City in Changsha, China, a 57-story skyscraper, was constructed in just 19 days using prefabricated materials.

The Oldest Living Tree
A bristlecone pine in California, nicknamed "Methuselah," is estimated to be over 4,800 years old, making it older than most ancient civilizations.

The Largest Diamond Ever Found
The Cullinan Diamond, discovered in South Africa in 1905, weighed an astonishing 3,106 carats before being cut into smaller gems.

The Heaviest Human
Jon Brower Minnoch weighed a staggering 1,400 pounds at his peak, holding the record for the heaviest person ever recorded.

The Longest Recorded Flight by a Chicken
A chicken managed to fly 13 seconds, covering a distance of 301.5 feet, defying the belief that chickens can't fly.

The Largest Snowflake Ever Recorded
In 1887, a snowflake measuring 15 inches wide was reported in Fort Keogh, Montana.

The Longest Time a Person Has Held Their Breath
Budimir Šobat set the record in 2021 by holding his breath for 24 minutes and 37 seconds.

The Largest Human Gathering
The Kumbh Mela festival in India drew over 50 million people in a single day in 2013, creating the largest human congregation in history.

The Most Books Written by One Person
L. Ron Hubbard, founder of Scientology, wrote 1,084 books, setting the record for the most published works by a single author.

The Largest Pizza Ever Made
In 2012, a pizza measuring 13,580 square feet was baked in Rome, requiring over 9,000 pounds of flour and 4,400 pounds of cheese.

The Longest Distance Walked Without Stopping
George Meegan walked 19,019 miles from Tierra del Fuego, Argentina, to Alaska between 1977 and 1983.

The Most Lightning Strikes Survived
Park ranger Roy Sullivan was struck by lightning seven times between 1942 and 1977, earning him the nickname "Human Lightning Rod."

The World's Longest Fingernail on a Single Hand
Shridhar Chillal of India grew his nails to a total length of 29 feet on one hand before cutting them in 2018 after 66 years.

The Largest Indoor Waterfall
Singapore's Jewel Changi Airport features a 131-foot-tall indoor waterfall, defying engineering expectations.

The Longest Recorded Lifespan
Jeanne Calment lived to be 122 years and 164 days old, a record that has yet to be surpassed.

The Fastest Speed Achieved by a Human on Land
Usain Bolt set the world record for the 100 meters at 9.58 seconds in 2009, reaching a top speed of 27.8 mph.

The Most Durable Light Bulb
The Centennial Light in California has been burning for over 120 years, defying expectations of bulb longevity.

The Largest Rubik's Cube
A Rubik's Cube measuring 6.5 feet on each side and weighing over 1,000 pounds holds the record for the largest functional cube.

The Smallest Dog Ever
A Chihuahua named Milly measures just 3.8 inches tall, making her the smallest dog on record.

The Largest Bouquet of Flowers
In 2005, a bouquet containing 156,940 roses was presented in India, weighing over 3,000 pounds.

The World's Largest Cave
Hang Son Doong in Vietnam is so vast it contains a river, jungle, and its own weather system inside.

The Most Body Modifications
Rolf Buchholz of Germany holds the record with over 516 body modifications, including piercings, tattoos, and implants.

The Most Expensive Painting Ever Sold
Leonardo da Vinci's *Salvator Mundi* sold for $450.3 million in 2017, a record-breaking price for any artwork.

The Longest-Ever Tennis Match
John Isner and Nicolas Mahut played a match at Wimbledon in 2010 that lasted 11 hours and 5 minutes over three days.

The Heaviest Aircraft Ever Built
The Antonov An-225, weighing 710 tons fully loaded, holds the record for the heaviest aircraft ever constructed.

The Tallest Man Ever
Robert Wadlow, standing at 8 feet 11 inches, holds the record for the tallest human in history.

The World's Longest Beard
In 1927, Hans Langseth's beard measured an incredible 17 feet 6 inches long.

The Most Expensive Coffee
Kopi Luwak, made from beans digested and excreted by civet cats, can cost up to $600 per pound.

The World's Longest Train Journey
The Trans-Siberian Railway covers 5,772 miles, stretching across eight time zones from Moscow to Vladivostok.

The Longest Hair on a Person
Xie Qiuping of China holds the record for the longest hair, measuring 18 feet 5 inches.

The Largest Watermelon Ever Grown
Chris Kent grew a watermelon weighing 350.5 pounds, setting the world record in 2013.

The Deepest Pool in the World
Deep Dive Dubai is 196 feet deep, featuring a sunken city theme for divers to explore.

The Most Push-Ups in 24 Hours
Charles Servizio completed 46,001 push-ups in a single day, setting the ultimate endurance record.

The Most Tattoos in 24 Hours
Hollis Cantrell set the record in 2008, tattooing 801 designs on volunteers in a single day.

The Heaviest Pumpkin
Mathias Willemijns grew a pumpkin weighing 2,624 pounds, the heaviest ever recorded.

The Largest Wave Ever Surfed
In 2020, Maya Gabeira surfed a wave measuring 73.5 feet in Nazaré, Portugal, breaking her own record.

The Largest Natural Mirror
Bolivia's Salar de Uyuni, a salt flat, becomes the world's largest mirror when covered with water during the rainy season.

The Coldest Place on Earth
Antarctica's Dome Fuji recorded a temperature of -144°F (-98°C), the lowest ever measured.

The Most Expensive Comic Book
Action Comics No. 1, featuring Superman's debut, sold for $3.25 million in 2021.

The Longest Pizza Ever Made
In 2017, a team in California created a pizza stretching 6,333 feet, feeding thousands of people.

The Deepest Cave in the World
The Veryovkina Cave in Georgia reaches a depth of 7,257 feet, making it the deepest known cave.

The Oldest Message in a Bottle
In 2018, a bottle containing a message dated 1886 was found on an Australian beach, making it the oldest message ever recovered.

The World's Fastest Roller Coaster
The *Formula Rossa* in Abu Dhabi reaches speeds of 149 mph, simulating the thrill of Formula 1 racing.

The Most Expensive Cheese
Pule cheese, made from Balkan donkey milk, costs over $1,000 per pound due to its rarity and complex production process.

The World's Longest Tongue
Nick Stoeberl's tongue measures 3.97 inches from tip to lip, earning him a spot in the record books.

The Largest Book Ever Published
The *Klencke Atlas*, measuring 6 x 7.5 feet, is so large it requires multiple people to turn its pages.

The World's Largest Egg
A fossilized egg from an extinct elephant bird weighed nearly 2,000 grams, dwarfing even ostrich eggs.

The Most Ice Cream Scoops Balanced on a Cone
Dimitri Panciera set the record by balancing 125 scoops on a single cone without it toppling.

The Tallest Mountain on Earth (Base to Summit)
While Everest is the tallest above sea level, Mauna Kea in Hawaii measures over 33,500 feet from its base on the ocean floor.

The Longest Continuous Applause
An audience in Germany applauded pianist Igor Levit for 20 minutes and 45 seconds after his performance in 2016.

The Largest Ball of Paint
Michael Carmichael in Indiana started painting a baseball in 1977. It now weighs over 4,000 pounds with 25,000 layers of paint.

The Most Bees on a Person
She Ping of China covered his body with 1.1 million bees, weighing approximately 240 pounds, in 2014.

The World's Longest Beard on a Living Person
Sarwan Singh's beard measures over 8 feet long, making him a living legend.

The Most Words Typed in a Minute
Barbara Blackburn holds the record for typing 212 words in one minute on a Dvorak keyboard.

The Largest Collection of Rubber Ducks
Charlotte Lee has amassed over 9,000 unique rubber ducks, making her the official queen of quackers.

The Longest Subway System
The Shanghai Metro stretches 803 miles, making it the longest urban transit system in the world.

The Most Tattoos on a Senior Citizen
Isobel Varley, the most tattooed senior woman, had over 93% of her body covered in tattoos before her death.

The Longest Time Spinning a Basketball
Thomas Kohnert set the record by spinning a basketball on his finger for 4 hours and 15 seconds in 2006.

The Most National Flags Flown in One Place
In 2012, 273 flags were raised simultaneously in Kuwait, representing every United Nations member.

The Heaviest Onion
Tony Glover grew an onion weighing 18 pounds and 11 ounces, breaking the record in 2014.

The World's Largest Chocolate Bar
Created in the UK in 2011, this chocolate bar weighed over 12,000 pounds and measured 13 feet long.

The Most Cockroaches Eaten
Ken Edwards consumed 36 live cockroaches in one minute in 2001, setting a stomach-churning record.

The Longest Underwater Walk on a Single Breath
Carlos Coste walked 316 feet on the ocean floor in 2016, holding his breath the entire time.

The Most Expensive Perfume
Shumukh, a luxury perfume from Dubai, costs $1.3 million and features diamond-encrusted packaging.

The Largest Collection of Comic Books
Bob Bretall owns over 140,000 unique comic books, making him the ultimate collector.

The Longest Ice Bath
Josef Koeberl stayed submerged in ice for 2 hours, 30 minutes, and 57 seconds, setting a chilling record.

The Most Lit Candles on a Birthday Cake
In 2016, a cake with 72,585 lit candles celebrated the birthday of Indian spiritual leader Sri Chinmoy.

The Largest Cup of Coffee
A 3,700-gallon cup of coffee was brewed in Colombia, breaking the record in 2019.

The World's Longest Sniper Kill
A Canadian sniper shot a target 2.14 miles away in 2017, achieving a nearly impossible feat.

The Tallest LEGO Tower
In 2015, a LEGO tower in Milan reached 114 feet, requiring hundreds of thousands of bricks.

The Longest Chess Game
A 1989 match in Belgrade lasted 269 moves and took over 20 hours to complete before ending in a draw.

The Largest Swimming Pool
The pool at San Alfonso del Mar in Chile spans over 20 acres and holds 66 million gallons of water.

The World's Longest Sausage
Made in Romania, this sausage stretched 38.99 miles, longer than a marathon.

The Heaviest Weight Lifted by a Human
Paul Anderson lifted 6,270 pounds in a backlift in 1957, setting a record that remains unbroken.

The Longest Time Balancing on One Foot
Arulanantham Suresh Joachim stood on one foot for 76 hours and 40 minutes in 1997.

The Most Expensive Car Ever Sold
A 1962 Ferrari 250 GTO sold for $70 million in 2018, making it the priciest car in history.

The Largest Cake Ever Baked
In 2008, a 150,000-pound cake was created in Las Vegas, enough to feed over 50,000 people.

The Longest Freefall Skydive
Alan Eustace jumped from 135,889 feet in 2014, breaking the sound barrier during his descent.

The World's Longest River
The Nile stretches 4,132 miles, narrowly edging out the Amazon for the title of the world's longest river.

The Most Pearls on a Wedding Dress
A Pakistani bride's dress was adorned with 100,000 pearls, setting a record for opulence.

The Largest Rubber Band Ball
Joel Waul created a ball weighing 9,032 pounds and measuring over 6 feet in diameter.

The Longest Career as a Waiter
Walter Orthmann worked at the same company in Brazil for over 80 years, setting the record for the longest career at a single business.

The Most People Inside a Soap Bubble
In 2016, 275 people stood inside a single soap bubble created by a team in Vietnam.

The Heaviest Vehicle Pulled by a Human
Rev. Kevin Fast pulled a 416,299-pound plane in 2009, showcasing superhuman strength.

The Longest Time Playing a Video Game
Okan Kaya played *Call of Duty: Black Ops II* for 135 hours straight, setting the marathon gaming record.

The World's Oldest Pair of Shoes
A 5,500-year-old leather shoe was discovered in an Armenian cave, perfectly preserved by natural conditions.

The Largest Human Mattress Dominoes
In 2016, 1,200 people toppled in succession on mattresses in Shanghai, setting a quirky record.

The Most Tattoos in a Lifetime
Lucky Diamond Rich has over 200% of his body tattooed, with some areas inked multiple times.

The Longest Marathon Hug
Two friends, Ron O'Neil and Theresa Kerr, hugged for 32 hours in 2010 to set this heartwarming record.

The Largest Domino Display
A team in Germany arranged 4,491,863 dominoes in 2017, toppling them all in a stunning chain reaction.

The Most Tattoos Done in 24 Hours by One Artist
Hollis Cantrell completed 801 tattoos in a single day in 2008, breaking the endurance record.

The Longest Time Living with a Bullet in the Head
William Lawlis Pace survived for 94 years with a bullet lodged in his head after a childhood accident.

The World's Largest Sundial
The Jantar Mantar in Jaipur, India, is a functioning sundial measuring 73 feet tall, built in 1738.

The Most Expensive Sneakers Ever Sold
A pair of Kanye West's *Nike Air Yeezy 1* sneakers sold for $1.8 million in 2021.

The Heaviest Weight Dangled from a Human Skull
John Evans balanced a 187-pound car on his head for 33 seconds in 1999.

The World's Largest Cheeseburger
A 2,014-pound cheeseburger was cooked in Minnesota in 2012, complete with a 60-pound bun and 40 pounds of cheese.

The Most Jumps Over a Moving Car
Alister Grey performed 10 leaps over a moving car in 2015, setting an extraordinary record.

The Longest Fingernails on a Single Hand
Shridhar Chillal grew nails on his left hand to a combined length of over 29 feet before cutting them in 2018.

The Longest Continuous High-Five Chain
In 2013, 14,372 people high-fived in a continuous line at an event in Canada.

The Largest Collection of Funko Pop Figures
David Mebane owns over 8,000 unique Funko Pop figurines, earning him a Guinness World Record.

The Longest Recorded Burp
Micheal Fogerty let out a burp lasting 1 minute and 13 seconds in 2009, solidifying his place in burping history.

The Most Coconuts Smashed with a Bare Hand in One Minute
Keshab Swain crushed 118 coconuts with his bare hand in 2011.

The Largest Gathering of People Dressed as Smurfs
In 2019, 2,762 people dressed as Smurfs in Germany, setting a whimsical record.

The World's Oldest Piece of Chewing Gum
A 9,000-year-old piece of birch bark tar gum was discovered in Sweden, still bearing human teeth marks.

The Largest Collection of Star Wars Memorabilia
Steve Sansweet owns over 500,000 *Star Wars* items, making his home, Rancho Obi-Wan, a fan's dream.

The Most Expensive Wedding
Vanisha Mittal, daughter of an Indian steel tycoon, had a $66 million wedding that included six days of celebrations across France.

The Longest Time Spent Buried Alive
Zdenek Zahradka survived 10 days buried in a coffin with no food, only a small breathing tube.

The Most Jello Eaten with Chopsticks in One Minute
Andre Ortolf consumed 716 grams of jello using chopsticks in under 60 seconds in 2017.

The World's Smallest Bird
The bee hummingbird, native to Cuba, weighs less than 2 grams and measures just 2 inches long.

The Longest Human Tunnel Skated Through by a Dog
In 2020, a dog named Otto skated through the legs of 30 people standing in a row, setting this adorable record.

The Largest Ball of Human Hair
Created by Ripley's Believe It or Not!, the ball weighs over 225 pounds and continues to grow as people contribute hair.

The Most Balloons Popped by a Dog in One Minute
An energetic dog named Twinkie popped 100 balloons in just 39.08 seconds in 2016.

The Largest Ice Cream Sundae

In 1988, a 54,917-pound sundae was created in Edmonton, Canada, requiring over 5,000 gallons of ice cream.

The Most Grapes Caught in the Mouth in One Minute

Ashrita Furman caught 86 grapes tossed from a distance in 2019.

The Largest Sandcastle Ever Built

In 2021, a team in Denmark constructed a sandcastle 69 feet tall, requiring nearly 5,000 tons of sand.

The Most Pancakes Flipped in One Hour

Ross McCurdy flipped 1,092 pancakes in just one hour in 2016, setting a sizzling record.

The Fastest Marathon Dressed as a Fruit

Andrew Lawrence completed the London Marathon dressed as a banana in 2 hours, 47 minutes, and 41 seconds.

The Largest Bubble Blown from Chewing Gum

Chad Fell blew a bubble measuring 20 inches in diameter without using his hands in 2004.

FICTIONAL FACTS

Fun truths about fictional worlds and how they relate to real life.

Sherlock Holmes never said, "Elementary, my dear Watson."
The iconic phrase, often associated with the world's most famous detective, does not appear in any of Sir Arthur Conan Doyle's stories.

Frankenstein is the doctor, not the monster.
Many people mistakenly call the creature "Frankenstein," but that's the name of its creator, Victor Frankenstein.

Walt Disney didn't create Mickey Mouse.
The initial concept for Mickey Mouse was created by Ub Iwerks, one of Disney's top animators, though Disney added his own creative touches.

Dracula wasn't the first vampire story.
Before Bram Stoker's *Dracula*, John Polidori's *The Vampyre* introduced readers to a sophisticated bloodsucker in 1819.

Captain Kirk never said, "Beam me up, Scotty."
Though often quoted, this phrase was never actually spoken in *Star Trek*. Variations of it appear, but not the exact line.

Santa Claus wasn't always jolly and red.
Coca-Cola popularized Santa's modern image in the 1930s. Before that, he appeared in various forms, including as a stern, bishop-like figure.

The Wicked Witch of the West wasn't always green.
In L. Frank Baum's original *The Wizard of Oz*, the Wicked Witch was not described as green. That detail came from the 1939 film.

The Great Wall of China is not visible from space.
Despite popular belief, astronauts cannot see the wall with the naked eye due to its thin structure and color blending with the landscape.

Robin Hood wasn't always a hero.
Early tales depict Robin Hood as a rogue who stole from anyone, not just the rich, before evolving into the noble outlaw we know today.

James Bond's iconic drink order is wrong.
While Bond often orders a "vodka martini, shaken, not stirred," martinis are traditionally stirred to avoid diluting the drink.

Tarzan never said, "Me Tarzan, you Jane."
This famous line never appears in Edgar Rice Burroughs' books or the early films, becoming a misquote over time.

The three witches in *Macbeth* never say "Double, double, toil and trouble."
They chant, "Double, double, toil and trouble; Fire burn, and cauldron bubble," making the common phrase incomplete.

Marie Antoinette didn't say, "Let them eat cake."
The infamous line attributed to the French queen was likely propaganda, as there's no evidence she ever said it.

George Washington didn't chop down a cherry tree.
The story about young George admitting, "I cannot tell a lie," was a fictional tale created by his biographer.

The original Cinderella slippers weren't made of glass.
In some early versions of the story, Cinderella's slippers were made of fur. The change to glass may have been a translation error.

Sherlock Holmes' hat isn't described in the books.
The deerstalker hat associated with Holmes was added by illustrators and wasn't mentioned in Conan Doyle's original works.

Bigfoot originated from a hoax.
The modern image of Bigfoot gained traction after a 1958 newspaper published a story about suspicious footprints, later revealed to be fake.

The myth of Atlantis started as philosophy.
Plato described Atlantis as an allegory, but it has since been taken literally by many as an actual lost city.

Jules Verne predicted modern technology.
In *From the Earth to the Moon* (1865), Verne described a moon mission with remarkable accuracy, foreshadowing NASA's Apollo program.

The Death Star's exhaust port wasn't a mistake.
In *Rogue One: A Star Wars Story*, it's revealed that the exhaust port was a deliberate design flaw added by an engineer to sabotage the Empire.

Shakespeare didn't invent Romeo and Juliet.
The tragic tale was based on an Italian story, and Shakespeare adapted it into his famous play.

Vikings didn't wear horned helmets.
The popular image of Viking warriors wearing horned helmets originated in 19th-century opera costumes, not historical evidence.

Einstein didn't fail math.
Contrary to popular myth, Albert Einstein excelled in mathematics as a child and was always a top student.

Zombies originated from Haitian folklore.
The concept of the undead was part of Haitian Vodou traditions long before
Hollywood turned zombies into flesh-eating monsters.

Napoleon wasn't short.
Napoleon's height was average for his time, but the British perpetuated the myth of
his short stature to mock him.

The phrase "Let there be light" wasn't Shakespearean.
While poetic, it originates from the Bible and not any of Shakespeare's works.

The Kraken wasn't a monster in early mythology.
Originally, the Kraken was described as a giant sea creature akin to a squid, not the
destructive beast popularized by modern stories.

The Mona Lisa isn't smiling.
Art experts have studied her expression extensively, concluding it's a neutral look
that creates the illusion of a smile.

Dr. Jekyll and Mr. Hyde were inspired by a real person.
Robert Louis Stevenson based the dual personality on a notorious Edinburgh figure
who led a double life.

The term "mad scientist" became popular from *Frankenstein*.
Mary Shelley's novel introduced the trope of a scientist driven by obsession,
inspiring countless similar characters.

Dragons appear in nearly every culture.
From Chinese mythology to European folklore, dragons symbolize power, wisdom,
or danger, despite no universal origin.

The Loch Ness Monster legend began with a photo hoax.
The famous "surgeon's photograph" of Nessie was revealed to be a staged image in 1994.

The Trojan Horse wasn't proven to exist.
The story of the wooden horse is primarily mythological, and no archaeological evidence confirms its use.

The Great Pyramid wasn't built by slaves.
Archaeological findings suggest that skilled laborers, not slaves, constructed the Egyptian pyramids.

The myth of werewolves has scientific roots.
Lycanthropy, a psychiatric condition, may have inspired early stories of people transforming into wolves.

Mermaids were mistaken manatees.
Early sailors reported seeing mermaids, but scientists believe they likely mistook manatees or dugongs for mythical creatures.

Shakespeare didn't write all his plays alone.
Many scholars believe Shakespeare collaborated with other playwrights, like Christopher Marlowe, on several works.

The Great Wall of China wasn't built in one go.
It's a series of walls constructed by different dynasties over centuries, not a single continuous project.

Medusa wasn't always a monster.
In Greek mythology, Medusa was originally a beautiful maiden cursed by Athena, turning her into a Gorgon.

Robin Hood's Merry Men weren't all merry.
Early tales describe some of his band as reluctant or even criminal, far from the loyal and jovial group we imagine today.

The Big Bad Wolf is older than *The Three Little Pigs*.
The wolf appears in Aesop's fables and other folklore long before becoming a house-huffing antagonist.

The Library of Alexandria wasn't burned in one event.
The destruction of the famous library likely occurred over several centuries, rather than a single catastrophic fire.

King Arthur's Excalibur wasn't his first sword.
Arthur initially wielded the sword Caliburn, which was later replaced by the more famous Excalibur.

Aladdin wasn't originally set in the Middle East.
The story from *One Thousand and One Nights* was likely added later by a French translator and originally set in China.

The Bermuda Triangle is mostly myth.
Most incidents attributed to the Bermuda Triangle have reasonable explanations, with no more disappearances than other heavily traveled areas.

Dracula was inspired by folklore, not Vlad the Impaler.
Bram Stoker drew on vampire myths from Eastern Europe, but the connection to Vlad was likely added later by historians.

The Pied Piper's story has historical roots.
It's believed to be based on a real event where many children from Hamelin disappeared, possibly due to disease or migration.

The genie in *Aladdin* didn't always grant three wishes.
Early versions of the story had the genie grant unlimited wishes, but later adaptations added the three-wish limit.

The Moon has been a literary muse for millennia.
Before space exploration, poets and authors imagined it as a land of gods, cheese, or magical creatures.

The idea of mermaids predates written history.
Cave paintings from over 30,000 years ago depict half-human, half-fish figures.

Dragons in Eastern and Western mythology are vastly different.
While Western dragons are often fire-breathing villains, Eastern dragons are wise, benevolent creatures associated with water.

The concept of zombies comes from Haitian Vodou.
The idea of the undead originated from rituals involving reanimated corpses under a sorcerer's control.

The concept of a utopia wasn't always positive.
Thomas More's original *Utopia* describes a fictional society that raises questions about perfection rather than celebrating it.

The Minotaur myth reflects ancient labyrinth rituals.
The story of Theseus and the Minotaur likely symbolizes rites of passage tied to Crete's labyrinthine palace architecture.

The Norse apocalypse, Ragnarök, ends with rebirth.
In Norse mythology, the end of the world isn't final—after Ragnarök, a new world emerges from the ashes.

The Holy Grail wasn't always a cup.
Early legends describe the Grail as a dish or stone before it became associated with the Last Supper chalice.

The Fountain of Youth myth is older than Ponce de León.
Tales of rejuvenating waters exist in many cultures, including ancient Greece and China, long before Ponce's quest.

The Headless Horseman legend isn't unique to America.
Variations of the headless specter appear in Irish, German, and Scandinavian folklore.

The Trojan Horse story is likely a metaphor.
Historians suggest the wooden horse could symbolize a siege engine or a clever deception rather than an actual giant structure.

The idea of cursed mummies is Victorian.
The notion that mummies bring curses gained popularity in 19th-century fiction, not ancient Egyptian beliefs.

King Midas's golden touch was a cautionary tale.
The Greek myth warns against greed, as Midas couldn't eat or touch loved ones without turning them to gold.

Atlantis may have been inspired by a volcanic eruption.
The myth of Atlantis could be based on the destruction of the Minoan civilization on the island of Thera.

Shangri-La is entirely fictional.
James Hilton invented the mystical land of Shangri-La in his 1933 novel *Lost Horizon*, though it's often linked to real Himalayan locations.

The werewolf legend has ancient roots.
The earliest werewolf story comes from *The Epic of Gilgamesh*, where a man is transformed into a wolf as punishment.

The phrase "Open Sesame" comes from Arabic.
In *Ali Baba and the Forty Thieves*, the magical phrase likely refers to sesame seeds, which burst open when ripe.

The Cheshire Cat's grin predates *Alice in Wonderland*.
The phrase "grinning like a Cheshire Cat" was a common saying in 18th-century England, long before Lewis Carroll's book.

The Yeti legend has cultural variations.
In the Himalayas, the Yeti is a protector of nature, while Western depictions often portray it as a monster.

The phoenix myth exists in many cultures.
From the Greek phoenix to the Chinese fenghuang, myths about a reborn bird span cultures and time periods.

The idea of elves has evolved over centuries.
In early folklore, elves were mischievous or even dangerous, far from the helpful or ethereal beings of modern tales.

Bigfoot myths date back to indigenous stories.
Native American legends describe a Sasquatch-like creature long before modern sightings.

The legend of Jack-o'-lanterns comes from Irish folklore.
The story of Stingy Jack involves a trickster cursed to wander the earth with a glowing ember inside a carved turnip.

The myth of fairies as tiny creatures is Victorian.
Earlier folklore described fairies as human-sized beings, sometimes indistinguishable from people.

The phrase "Bloody Mary" originates from folklore.
The mirror-based legend likely stems from divination rituals in the 18th and 19th centuries.

The flying carpet myth predates *Aladdin*.
Tales of magical flying carpets appear in ancient Persian and Indian folklore long before they became part of the *Arabian Nights*.

The phrase "Curiosity killed the cat" is incomplete.
The full version is "Curiosity killed the cat, but satisfaction brought it back," giving the proverb a more positive twist.

The Tooth Fairy tradition is a modern invention.
Though similar customs exist worldwide, the specific idea of the Tooth Fairy leaving money under a pillow began in early 20th-century America.

The Kraken wasn't always destructive.
In early Scandinavian folklore, the Kraken was thought to help fishermen by scaring fish into their nets.

The idea of Martians predates modern astronomy.
In 1877, Italian astronomer Giovanni Schiaparelli observed "canali" (channels) on Mars, mistranslated as "canals," sparking theories of intelligent life.

Cinderella's story has over 500 versions.
Her tale appears in cultures worldwide, with variations including Chinese, African, and Native American versions.

The Sword in the Stone isn't Excalibur.
In Arthurian legend, the Sword in the Stone and Excalibur are separate weapons, with the latter given to Arthur by the Lady of the Lake.

The Easter Bunny is rooted in pagan traditions.
The hare was a symbol of fertility in ancient European spring festivals, long before being associated with Easter.

The phrase "Sleeping Beauty" didn't exist in the original tale.
The earliest versions of the story referred to her as Talia or Briar Rose, with "Sleeping Beauty" added in later retellings.

The Cyclops myth may have been inspired by fossils.
Ancient Greeks may have mistaken the skulls of extinct elephants, with large nasal cavities, for giant, one-eyed creatures.

The Pied Piper legend may symbolize the plague.
The disappearance of the children of Hamelin could represent a plague outbreak, with the Piper as a metaphor for death.

The idea of leprechauns as tiny men is modern.
Early Irish folklore described leprechauns as human-sized cobblers, not the small, mischievous figures we know today.

Medusa's gaze wasn't always petrifying.
In some myths, Medusa's gaze represented wisdom or protection, not just destruction.

The werewolf legend has ties to medical conditions.
Porphyria and hypertrichosis, rare conditions causing hair growth and sensitivity to light, may have inspired werewolf stories.

The basilisk myth may come from cobras.
The basilisk's description in European lore matches the venomous spitting cobras of Africa and Asia.

The Phoenix myth inspired Harry Potter's Fawkes.
J.K. Rowling's depiction of Fawkes, Dumbledore's loyal phoenix, borrows heavily from the ancient rebirth mythology.

The term "Blackbeard" was a propaganda tool.
Edward Teach cultivated his fearsome pirate image by lighting fuses in his beard, though he was reportedly polite in person.

Mermaids were once seen as omens of disaster.
Sailors believed spotting a mermaid foretold shipwrecks, blending awe with fear in maritime lore.

The Cheshire Cat's grin symbolizes wisdom.
In *Alice in Wonderland*, the cat's enigmatic smile reflects riddles and puzzles, mirroring Alice's journey of discovery.

RANDOM WONDERS

Fascinating miscellanea

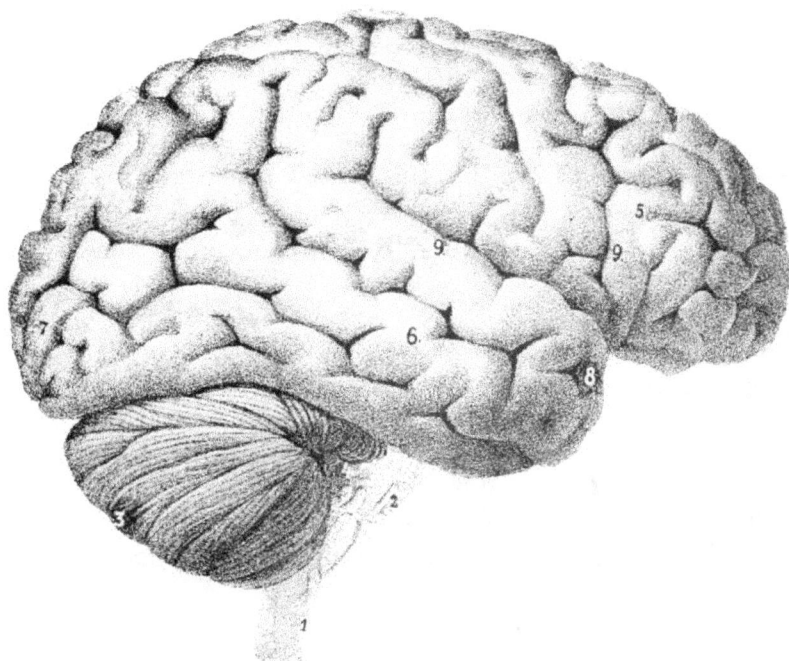

The Eiffel Tower can grow taller.
In the summer, the metal structure expands due to heat, making the Eiffel Tower about 6 inches taller.

Octopuses have three hearts.
Two pump blood to the gills, while the third pumps it to the rest of the body. When they swim, the main heart temporarily stops.

There's a species of jellyfish that is biologically immortal.
The *Turritopsis dohrnii* can revert its cells to an earlier stage of life, effectively avoiding death by old age.

Sloths can hold their breath longer than dolphins.
By slowing their heart rate, sloths can hold their breath for up to 40 minutes, while dolphins typically last about 10 minutes.

There's a basketball court in the U.S. Supreme Court building.
Located on the top floor, it's nicknamed "The Highest Court in the Land."

A group of flamingos is called a "flamboyance."
The fitting term reflects their bright colors and dramatic behavior.

You can't hum while holding your nose.
Try it—you'll find that without the passage of air, humming becomes impossible.

A blue whale's heart is the size of a small car.
It weighs around 400 pounds and pumps 60 gallons of blood with each beat.

The hottest chili pepper can kill you.
The Carolina Reaper is so spicy that eating too much can cause a lethal reaction by constricting airways.

There's a McDonald's in every continent except Antarctica.
Even remote places like Siberia and the Amazon have Golden Arches, but Antarctica remains Mc-free.

Your stomach gets a new lining every 3-4 days.
This prevents the stomach from digesting itself due to its acidic environment.

The dot over a lowercase "i" and "j" is called a tittle.
This small but significant detail has a name rooted in Latin, meaning a small mark.

Penguins propose with pebbles.
Male penguins search for the perfect pebble to present to their mate during courtship.

There are more stars in the universe than grains of sand on Earth.
Scientists estimate there are roughly 10 sextillion stars, far exceeding Earth's sand grains.

The inventor of the Pringles can is buried in one.
Fred Baur, who created the iconic can, requested his ashes be placed in one as part of his burial.

Humans share 60% of their DNA with bananas.
Though vastly different species, the genetic overlap is a testament to life's common origins.

A day on Saturn lasts just 10 hours.
The planet's rapid rotation creates one of the shortest days in the solar system.

A cockroach can live for weeks without its head.
Cockroaches can survive decapitation due to their decentralized nervous system and ability to breathe through spiracles.

Mount Everest grows every year.
Due to tectonic activity, the world's tallest mountain increases in height by about 4 millimeters annually.

The shortest war in history lasted 38 minutes.
In 1896, the Anglo-Zanzibar War ended almost as quickly as it began.

Scotland has 421 words for "snow."
Terms like "sneesl" (to begin to rain or snow) showcase the rich linguistic history of Scots.

Humans are the only animals that blush.
Blushing is a uniquely human reaction triggered by embarrassment or shame.

The Eiffel Tower was once yellow.
The iconic structure has sported several colors over the years, including red, brown, and yellow.

The longest hiccuping spree lasted 68 years.
Charles Osborne hiccupped non-stop from 1922 to 1990, earning a spot in medical history.

Butterflies taste with their feet.
Their taste sensors are located on their feet, allowing them to identify suitable plants for laying eggs.

A single strand of spaghetti is called a spaghetto.
The term comes from the Italian singular form, highlighting how every piece has its own name.

Rainbows can appear at night.
Known as "moonbows," these rare phenomena occur when moonlight refracts through water droplets.

Water can boil and freeze at the same time.
This phenomenon, called the triple point, occurs under specific pressure and temperature conditions.

Earth is the only planet not named after a god.
All other planets in the solar system are named after Roman or Greek deities.

The longest place name in the world is 85 letters long.
It's a hill in New Zealand called Taumatawhakatangihangakoauauotamateaturipukakapikimaungahoronukupokaiwhe nuakitanatahu.

A cloud can weigh more than a million pounds.
Despite their fluffy appearance, clouds are made of tiny water droplets that add up to massive weight.

Cows have best friends.
Studies show that cows form close bonds and get stressed when separated from their companions.

The Statue of Liberty's fingernails are 8 feet long.
The copper statue's hands are proportional to her massive height of 151 feet.

The human brain generates enough electricity to power a lightbulb.
It produces about 20 watts of electrical energy, even while resting.

A year on Neptune lasts 165 Earth years.
Neptune takes so long to orbit the Sun that it has completed only one orbit since its discovery in 1846.

The heart of a blue whale is as big as a car.
It weighs around 400 pounds and pumps 60 gallons of blood per beat.

Antarctica is the largest desert in the world.
Despite its icy terrain, Antarctica qualifies as a desert due to its minimal precipitation.

Your body contains enough iron to make a small nail.
If all the iron in your body were collected, it could form a 3-inch nail.

There's a species of starfish that can regrow its entire body.
The Linckia starfish can regenerate from a single arm as long as the central disk is intact.

It rains diamonds on Jupiter and Saturn.
Extreme pressure in the atmospheres of these planets can compress carbon into diamond rain.

Giraffes only need 5-30 minutes of sleep a day.
They take short naps standing up and rarely lie down due to predators.

Earth's core is as hot as the Sun's surface.
The core reaches temperatures of up to 10,800°F, matching the Sun's outer layer.

Hot water freezes faster than cold water.
This phenomenon, known as the Mpemba effect, occurs under certain conditions, though scientists still debate why.

There's a planet made of solid diamond.
55 Cancri e, a planet 40 light-years away, is thought to be covered in diamond due to its carbon-rich composition.

A cockroach can live for a week without its head.
Cockroaches can survive decapitation, eventually dying from dehydration rather than injury.

Horses can't vomit.
Their unique digestive systems prevent them from throwing up, making certain foods and illnesses particularly dangerous.

Octopuses have blue blood.
Their blood contains copper-based hemocyanin instead of iron-based hemoglobin, giving it a blue color.

A bolt of lightning contains enough energy to toast 100,000 slices of bread.
Each strike releases up to a billion joules of energy, enough to power a household for weeks.

Bananas are naturally radioactive.
They contain potassium-40, a radioactive isotope, but the levels are far too low to be harmful.

The hottest temperature ever recorded on Earth was 134°F.
This record was set in Furnace Creek, California, in 1913.

Sloths can hold their breath longer than dolphins.
By slowing their heart rate, sloths can hold their breath for up to 40 minutes, compared to a dolphin's 10 minutes.

The Great Pyramid of Giza can focus electromagnetic energy.
Studies show that the pyramid can concentrate electromagnetic energy in its internal chambers and base.

The human nose can detect over 1 trillion scents.
Our sense of smell is far more powerful than previously thought, helping us identify an incredible variety of odors.

Earth's magnetic field is shifting.
The magnetic north pole moves approximately 25 miles a year, affecting navigation systems.

Cats can't taste sweetness.
Unlike humans, cats lack taste receptors for sweetness, which explains their indifference to sugary treats.

The longest recorded flight of a chicken lasted 13 seconds.
Though they're not known for flying, chickens can manage short bursts of air travel.

The Moon is drifting away from Earth.
The Moon moves about 1.5 inches farther from Earth each year, affecting tides and our planet's rotation over time.

A shrimp's heart is in its head.
The heart and other vital organs of a shrimp are located in its thorax, behind its head.

Humans share 98% of their DNA with chimpanzees.
This genetic similarity highlights our close evolutionary relationship with primates.

The Amazon rainforest produces 20% of the world's oxygen.
Known as the "lungs of the Earth," the rainforest plays a critical role in global oxygen production.

The Pacific Ocean is shrinking.
Tectonic plate movement causes the Pacific to decrease in size by about an inch each year.

A flea can jump 350 times its body length.
This makes fleas one of the most impressive jumpers in the animal kingdom, relative to size.

You're taller in the morning.
Gravity compresses the cartilage in your spine throughout the day, making you slightly shorter by evening.

Ants can lift objects 50 times their body weight.
Their incredible strength allows them to carry food and materials back to their colonies.

Your blood travels 12,000 miles a day.
In a single day, your heart pumps enough blood to travel the length of the U.S. coast-to-coast four times.

Some fish communicate by farting.
Herring release air bubbles from their swim bladders to communicate with one another.

A jellyfish is 95% water.
Despite their complex movements, jellyfish are mostly water, giving them their gelatinous appearance.

The shortest war in history lasted 38 minutes.
The Anglo-Zanzibar War of 1896 ended quickly when British forces overwhelmed Zanzibar's defenses.

The Eiffel Tower sways in the wind.
The metal structure can sway up to 6 inches on windy days without compromising its integrity.

Dolphins have names for each other.
They use unique whistles to identify and call out to specific members of their pod.

The Apollo Astronauts Left Mirrors on the Moon
These mirrors, placed during the Apollo missions, are still used today to measure the exact distance between the Earth and the Moon.

Venus is the Hottest Planet, Not Mercury
Despite being farther from the Sun, Venus's thick atmosphere traps heat, maintaining surface temperatures of around 900°F.

Sea Cucumbers Breathe Through Their Anuses
These ocean dwellers use their rectums to pump water in and out, extracting oxygen in the process.

There's a Lake in Tanzania That Turns Animals to Stone
Lake Natron's high alkalinity preserves animals that die in its waters, creating eerie, mummified remains.

You Can't Burp in Space
Without gravity, gas in your stomach doesn't separate from liquids, so burping isn't possible without also throwing up.

The Largest Living Organism is a Fungus
A honey fungus in Oregon spans over 2.4 miles underground, making it the largest organism by area on Earth.

CONCLUSION

And so, dear reader, we reach the end of our journey—a winding road paved with historical oddities, cosmic mysteries, and facts so bizarre they probably made you double-check that this isn't a work of fiction. If your brain feels a little fuller (and perhaps a tad overwhelmed), then my mission has been accomplished.

Throughout these pages, we've explored the unexplainable, the unbelievable, and the downright ridiculous. From sloths holding their breath longer than dolphins to octopus hearts taking a coffee break during swims, it's clear that the world is much weirder than any of us could have imagined. And that's just the tip of the iceberg! (Which, fun fact, contains 90% of its mass below water. You're welcome—one last bonus fact for the road.)

But why stop here? The universe is bursting with even more wonders waiting to be uncovered. Who knows what new discoveries or peculiarities tomorrow might bring? Maybe scientists will find life on a diamond planet, or perhaps someone will finally solve the mystery of why socks disappear in the dryer. Either way, it's comforting to know there will always be something fascinating to learn—or laugh about—if we keep our minds open.

As you close this book and return to the "normal" world, remember: the extraordinary is everywhere, often hiding in plain sight. So keep asking questions, stay curious, and don't be afraid to look at life from a different angle (even if it's upside-down like a sloth). And most importantly, the next time someone tries to one-up you at trivia night, just smile knowingly—you've got enough mind-blowing facts now to silence the whole room.

Thank you for taking this journey with me. It's been a wild ride through the weird and wonderful, and I hope it's left you as amazed and entertained as I was while assembling these gems of knowledge. Until next time, stay curious, stay weird, and always keep a spare banana handy—just in case you need to test your shared DNA.

DID
YOU KNOW?

A Collection of the Most Mind-Blowing Facts about Everything!